From the book...

Around ten o'clock in the morning Opa, my mother's dad, arrived. "Hello, rascal. I'm here to pick you up. You are going to stay with us for a while."
I wanted to ask him about Mom but somehow I couldn't. I was afraid.
"Opa, how long am I staying?"
"Maybe two or three days."
Oma had just made lunch when we arrived. She was toasting bread in the silver toaster. She had bought raisin rolls, my favorites.
After lunch, I asked Oma and Opa where Mom was.
"Oh, my God. You don't know?!" Oma exclaimed.
Opa moved closer to me.
"Your mother is dead," he said.
I put my head in my arms and started crying softly. I was not sad. I was alone.
"The funeral is Wednesday," Oma said. "Do you want to go?"
"No, I don't want to be there! People will be staring at me."
"That's okay," Opa said, "That's okay."
And he put his hand on my shoulder.

***

Dad didn't feel comfortable speaking about Mom except in general, abstract terms.
"She was a very good woman. She is with angels now."
He didn't like private, risky topics. He simply shut down, putting up a safety shield. If Hugo and I pushed too long he became angry, and would tell us he had his own privacy which we should respect. Often, Dad just stalked off, avoiding confrontation. He hated to be reminded of the bad things that happened. He never raised the topic. It became taboo inside our home. From the outside, our family must have looked just fine. Dad was the hard-working widower who had two nice boys. Dad liked it that way. He did not want too many people asking questions.

*To Andrea & Berry:
With gratitude for
your friendship!*
— August

She Is With Angels

My mother's suicide, a child's journey

***

August Swanenberg

Cross Cultural Publications, Inc.

Cross Roads Books

To Warren & Betsy:
With gratitude for
your friendship!

N. Nyu?

She Is With Angels

My mother's suicide, a child's journey

***

August Swanenberg

Copyright © 2001 by August Swanenberg

All rights reserved. Except for brief quotations in critical articles or reviews, no part of this book may be reproduced in any manner without prior written permission from the publisher: Cross Cultural Publications, P.O. Box 506, Notre Dame, IN 46556.

Printed in the United States of America. *First Edition*

Grateful acknowledgement is made for permission to reprint the lyrics of the song "White Rabbit," Copyright © Grace Slick. Used by permission. All rights reserved. Universal Music Publishing Group.

Pencil sketch on front cover by Charles Swanenberg
Cover art by Christine English

Library of Congress Catalogue Number: 2001 130 392
ISBN: 0-940121-60-3

Swanenberg, August.
She Is With Angels: My mother's suicide, a child's journey – 1st ed.

Published by Cross Cultural Publications, Inc., Cross Roads Books

To my wife, Julie, and to our children, Irene and Audrey

Contents

Prologue

1.	The Hoogeinde Home	1
2.	Kindergarten Treats	11
3.	Hugo's Bike	13
4.	Witness	15
5.	Last Day At Hoogeinde	18
6.	The New Town	30
7.	American Cornflakes	43
8.	A Special Mass	48
9.	Vacation In Lugano	51
10.	The Trip To Vught	61
11.	January 2, 1966	68
12.	Sherries And Camel Cigarettes	72
13.	At Home	75
14.	Remembrance Mass	78
15.	The Sounds Of Spoons	80
16.	The Trip To Italy	86
17.	Moving On	89
18.	The New School	94

19. Final Exam	101
20. College	105
21. A Goodbye	111
22. One Last Sign	134
23. The Old Home	138
24. The Flight Home	141

Epilogue

Acknowledgements

SUPPLEMENT

Appendix 1: Suicide Survivor Organizations (U.S. and Canada)

Appendix 2: Resources for Information

PROLOGUE

My mother killed herself when I was ten years old.
After years of mental illness, she slowly lost touch with her family and with herself.
I tried hard to forget.
First came the silence. My dad, my brother and I didn't talk about what happened. The taboo of suicide was strong.
But I didn't forget.
Later, I started asking Dad questions. He never answered.
Years passed but the old images didn't fade: my mother's sleepless nights, her suicide attempts, the green bottle of hydrochloric acid, and Grandpa putting his hand on my shoulder, telling me she had died.
Thirty-five years later, I want to share my story: *She Is With Angels*

She Is With Angels is written for survivors of suicide and for those who have experienced mental illness, either first hand or through friends or family members.
Each year, 32,000 people die from suicide in the U.S., more than from murder. Suicide is the leading cause of death among adolescents. A suicide occurs every 15 minutes in the U.S. and it is estimated that an attempt is made about once a minute. The taboo on suicide is one of the strongest in our society.
TIME Magazine reported that mental depression will become the second leading cause of death in the next 20 years (currently, it is ranked fourth.) More than 40 million Americans will suffer an episode of depression or mania during their lifetimes. One in four families will directly feel the impact. Despite these large numbers, the societal taboo surrounding mental illness remains powerful.

If my story can help you to overcome taboos affecting you or your family I will be grateful. I sincerely wish that this book may provide comfort and hope on *your* journey.

1

The Hoogeinde Home

"Look, he is beautiful."
The baby's short cry filled the room. The midwife handed the mother her new son.
"He has a nice bundle of hair," the mother said quietly and gently stroked the boy's hair.
She smiled at the yawning baby.
   It was one in the morning on Sunday. The birth had been quick and uneventful.
"Can Charles come in now to see him?" the mother asked.
The midwife opened the door to the hallway.
"It's a boy! They are fine," she announced to the father.
He walked into the room and smiled when he saw the baby.
"Oh, Riny, he looks great! His hair is much darker than Hugo's."
   He bent over, kissing his wife.
"Do you want me to wake up Hugo?" he asked.
"No. Let him sleep. He can see August in the morning."
They both looked at the baby, who was quiet and content.
"Riny, he is a Sunday child."
"Yes, he will be lucky in life."

I was born in the town of Tiel, The Netherlands.

Our home at Hoogeinde 5 was part of a distinguished row of houses just off Water Street, Tiel's main street. My parents could afford the house only because it needed work.

We had no bathtub or shower. On Saturday nights, Dad would take a gray metal tub from the basement and, with a clanking sound, place it on the kitchen floor. Then he used a bucket to fill the large tub with hot water from the kitchen sink. Taking turns, my brother Hugo and I would have our baths. The metal sides of the tub felt cold but I'd be comfortable after carefully sliding into the warm water. When the tips of my fingers were white and wrinkled I'd get out and wrap myself, shivering, in our large purple towel.

The kitchen in our house was small, dominated by the old black iron oven that we used as a heater. The oven was so heavy that not even Dad could move it.

When the kitchen needed heating, Mom used a rod to open one of the lids covering the burner holes of the oven. She'd put crumpled newspapers inside and throw in a burning match. After the newspapers caught fire she slid pieces of kindling into the oven. With flames shooting out of the burner hole she'd put the lid back: our kitchen furnace was on.

We weren't the only ones living at Hoogeinde 5.
One day, we were starting lunch in the kitchen. I looked forward to my sandwich with chocolate hail. Mom sat down next to me. As we began to eat, she suddenly screamed: "Charles, a mouse. Quick!"
My father jumped out of his chair. "OK, I saw it!" he said.
The mouse scurried under the wooden chest next to the oven. Dad quickly opened the chest, put his foot on the bottom board, and pressed hard, squishing the mouse under the board. Blood splashed onto the green linoleum floor next to me.
"What a mess!" Mom exclaimed.
My father quietly sat down and continued to eat.
I didn't want my sandwich with chocolate hail anymore.

Our attic was dusty and dark. Light came in through a tiny window in the top of the roof. When it was quiet you could hear the sound of mice behind the large suitcases stacked in the back. I'd often go up to check if a mouse had gotten caught in one of our traps. Hugo, who was five years older, told me that ghosts gathered in the attic at night. I didn't believe him but when I woke up in the middle of the night I always listened for sounds from upstairs. Sometimes I heard the light sound of mice walking around and I pretended they were Hugo's ghosts.

Hugo looked like Dad's father, Grandpa Swanenberg. Dad was fond of showing the black and white photograph of Grandpa in his early twenties, sitting at his desk.

"The spitting image of Hugo, isn't it?" he said. The man at the desk was wearing old-fashioned clothes but looked just like Hugo: blond hair, same finely shaped mouth and small nose. I found it eerie, but Hugo liked it.

"Grandpa was a handsome man," Dad continued. "He liked to shop at the best stores in Tiel or Den Bosch for his clothes. He was always the gentleman, using his walking stick, parading through the streets of Tiel. Some of the best-known people in town were his friends."

There was admiration in Dad's voice but I sensed he was totally different than his father. Dad was not going to parade through Tiel. He hardly left the house.

He ended stories about his father in the same way.

"I never really got to know him. I mostly spent time with Mom. My father expected a lot from me and from my younger brother Louis. Louis was his favorite because he fought with other boys and played soccer. Because I was the oldest I did my father's errands, delivering packages on my bike to clients as far away as Zoelen."

Dad put the photograph back on the mantle. He looked exhausted.

Dad ran his small photo developing business from our home. Upstairs, he had built a dark room and photo laboratory. Beige plastic tubes, stuffed with wires, were neatly organized in the corner. Dad was very good with electricity. The dark room had a small light hanging in a corner and was just big enough for him and his machine. To protect exposed film, a red cover over the light kept the room dark, like a permanent sunset. Dad was constantly hunched over the film, with the machine making its monotonous high-pitched clicks, picture after picture, and roll after roll. In the middle of the morning, he would come downstairs to take a break and smoke cigarettes. He washed his hands like a surgeon, applying soap two or three times, rubbing his hands carefully.

Dad was mostly bald, with only small patches of gray hair on his sides. His face was wrinkled and his cheeks were saggy. When I sat on his lap, I liked to take the skin of his cheeks between my fingers and stretch it out as far as I could. He didn't like to be touched, and I sensed that when I felt his cheeks, full of prickly white and gray stubble. Dad's left ear was longer than his right ear. He always got mad when I mentioned this. He would tell me to not make fun of him and he sounded serious.

Sometimes, I'd see a dark-brown piece of tobacco on his lips. His breath and his clothes always had the scent of Van Nelle Heavy tobacco.

After his morning break he would go up the stairs to start mixing fixation chemicals in the large plastic tub. Next to it, Dad hung his rolls of film negatives on a plastic wire. Silvery metal clamps at the bottom held down the curly strips. Sometimes I'd go up to watch him stir pictures in the green transparent fluid. I'd catch the sharp smell of the chemicals. They made the inside of my mouth dry and sticky. Dad warned me to stay away from the tub.

"Don't get too close, August. It's poisonous!" he'd say in a concerned voice.

"Dad, why do you need to do this mixing?" I asked.

"Oh, August, that's chemistry. I'll tell you later," he said, surprised by my interest.

Hugo said he knew what Dad was doing. He had read about it in a book on photography. Hugo was older; he knew about these things.

Hugo and I did not want to do Dad's work. It looked dreadful to us and Dad understood.

"If you do well in school you can choose whatever you want to be," he said. "With a University degree you'll be settled for life."

He made it sound like the promised land.

Every summer, trade union members nationwide went on vacation for two weeks. Dad's workload peaked when the large unions, Construction and Metal, returned from vacation. He called it the 'Season' and he worked seven days a week, from early morning to midnight. The Season went on for four full weeks.

Mom helped out in the Season, rinsing and drying developed pictures. She hovered for hours under a desk lamp, checking the gloss on the pictures. In a quick move, Mom would put her hair behind her ear so she could inspect pictures close to the light. She had dark brown hair, the same color as mine. Her eyes were brown, deeply set, with long eyebrows and together with her full soft-red lips they gave her a striking appearance. She looked thin and elegant in her light summer dresses. She had been an excellent swimmer and runner in high school.

Using the light, she tried to catch the pictures that didn't have a smooth shiny gloss. She then sorted the finished pictures by number to correspond with their order in each roll of film. On a busy day Mom would handle over a thousand pictures. It was hot in the house and she'd run out of time doing pictures, laundry, cooking and other chores. At the end of the Season, Mom was worn out. She had lost weight and her nice features were now hidden behind a tired look, protruding cheekbones and a slight hunch. She complained about her pale face, trying to catch the little sunshine left in late August and September.

Dad always felt happy at the end of the Season. Usually, business was good during the Season and he earned a nice income, enough to tide us over during the slow winter months.

When I turned five, my parents began sending me to a six-week overnight camp during the Season. They were too busy to keep an eye on me. I did not like camp because I wanted to play at home and explore our town with my friends. But my parents were strict. "You are too young to be here during the Season," they said.

Hugo, who was ten years old, could help around the house. So he was allowed to stay at home.

In late June, Aunt Netty or Aunt Fie, Mom's younger sisters, would drop me off at the start of camp in Driebergen, a train ride of forty minutes. Mom and Dad were already too busy with the Season to go themselves.

Aunt Netty worked at Daalderop, a large metal factory in Tiel. She smoked a lot, liked shopping for clothes and went to the hairdresser every Saturday morning. She earned enough to go on airplane vacations to Italy and Yugoslavia. Dad could get really mad about this. "Factory people are getting huge pensions and social security. I get nothing, having my own business." But Dad did not want to join Daalderop. He liked his independence.

When Aunt Netty was eighteen, she had met Johan, who was a housepainter. Within a year they were engaged. The engagement lasted for eight years. Twice, Johan painted a complete apartment for the newlyweds but Aunt Netty steadfastly refused to get married and move in. Finally, Johan had enough and broke off the engagement. "The white linens were already in the closet," my grandma, Oma, used to say. The linens were her engagement gift to the young couple. The first time I heard about this it had happened ten years earlier.

Still, it always sounded like yesterday's story. Aunt Netty had had an affair with her boss at Daalderop throughout her engagement with Johan. The boss had promised to divorce his wife in order to marry my aunt. That promise made my aunt reluctant to move in with housepainter Johan. The boss never divorced and Aunt Netty never married. Oma sometimes showed me Johan's picture. She had kept one around.

Aunt Fie was seven years younger than Aunt Netty. She worked at Dutch Railways in Utrecht, taking reservations over the phone and telex machine. Aunt Fie was planning to get her driver's license and buy a car. She loved Italy and spoke Italian quite well. Oma joked that she would end up marrying an Italian and leave Tiel.

Each year on the way to camp, I was quiet, feeling sad about leaving home. I put my head on the little train table and cried.
"August, do you see the hills? It looks so different here," Aunt Fie said.
I was listening to her but I kept sobbing.
"The forest starts here. You should see this," my aunt continued.
I stopped sniffing and looked up, staring out the window.
"August, it's beautiful here, isn't it?"
I nodded slightly. I didn't feel like crying any longer.
Aunt Fie smiled at me.
"You'll be back home before you know it," she said quietly.
The people in the train had stopped looking at us.

At camp I went along with the activities but I didn't like camp leaders who tried hard to involve me. In the first week, I was homesick but I didn't write home because I was still mad at my parents for sending me to camp. I also knew they were too busy to write back.

I looked forward to the trip to Ouwehand's Zoo in the nearby town of Rhenen. I loved walking around by myself, enjoying the shrieking macaws at the zoo's entrance, watching the polar bears eat their meat, and petting the goats.

Dad's Season ended four weeks later. Finally, I could go back home. Because my parents were still busy, my aunts would pick me up from camp. I was happy to see them and I enjoyed the train ride back to Tiel. The first day at home was like a party, because Mom had made special treats and cake. Everybody was extra nice to me. After that, it took a few days to get used to being home again.

The salon room in our house on Hoogeinde street was for guests and off-limits to Hugo and me. In the middle of the salon was our large couch with the pink pillows, embroidered with flowers. I loved bouncing on the big pillows.
"Dad, can I go into the salon, please?" I begged.
"No, August. The salon is our special place in the house. I don't want you to mess it up," Dad answered sternly.
"Did you have a salon when you were little?" I asked.
"Yes. I can show you an old picture."
"Neat!"

Dad was eager to show me his picture, getting up quickly to take it out of the desk drawer. He liked to talk about the old house. He rummaged in the drawer and found his picture. He proudly showed the faded, yellowish photograph to me.
"August, we used to live where the *Luxor* movie theater now is on Water Street. Our house was large. If I wanted to hide, I could simply disappear somewhere upstairs or, better yet, in the attic. I loved the attic."
The furniture in the salon was beautiful, especially the table with tiny wheels for serving coffee and tea. A lady servant in a white uniform stood next to it.
"Do you like it?" Dad asked.
"Yes, it looks very nice, Dad," I said, fascinated by the servant who seemed to be part of the furniture.
"How many servants did you have, Dad?"
"At one time we had five. Grandpa's business was booming in the 20's and he liked to live in style. My parents wore fashionable clothes, went to the theater, and often entertained at home."
"Why don't they live there anymore, Dad?"

"Well, August, business turned bad during the Depression in the 30's. People had less money and didn't want to spend as much on photography. When my dad couldn't afford his laboratory assistant anymore I had to leave the Art Academy and help out. And he had to sell the house."
"Too bad I can't see the *Luxor* house," I said.
"It was beautiful," he said quietly.
"Can I go look at the pictures in the salon, Dad?"
"O.K., August. But be careful," Dad said absent-mindedly.
I don't think he noticed that I left the room.

    I opened the hallway door to the salon. The sunlight coming in from the windows across the room made me squint. After I got used to the light, I went to the couch, kneeling down on a pillow to see Dad's baby picture up close. It was from 1915. The picture sat in an oval-shaped, ornamented white frame. Grandma Swanenberg, in her early twenties, was proudly holding her firstborn, my father, who was six months old. Grandpa had artfully retouched the black and white photograph by drawing Grandma's high-collared dress in blue and black pencil. Dad said that photographers in Grandpa's era were artists. "She was the prettiest woman in all of Tiel," Dad told me.
    The picture reminded him of World War I and he often told the story of the Royal Cavalry captain who boarded in their house. Near the end of the war, when my father was three years old, the captain took him to the stables at Hotel Telkamp, which had been commissioned by the Royal Cavalry.
"I can still smell the horses and the hay piled up everywhere," Dad said.
"The captain liked me and showed me around. At the end of our trip, he put me on his horse. It was huge."
    When the War ended, the captain's commission in Tiel was over. One early morning, he assembled his men in front of the house. Peering out the window of the salon room, Grandma and Dad waved as the company lined up their horses in formation and saluted before they moved out.
I didn't understand one picture in the salon. It was Mom and Dad's wedding picture: Mom was wearing a dark dress and a black beret. She was not wearing any white. Mom once told me that they didn't have much time to prepare for the wedding before Hugo was born. Mom never answered my questions

about the picture. Shrugging her shoulders, she'd just say she was busy and would leave the room.

Our only family group picture sat on a small table near the window. Christmas 1959. The tiny tree in the background was almost lost in the green curtains. The large size electric lights were bigger than the ornaments. I sat in the middle on my father's lap. Dad was wearing a dark jacket and his white suspenders showed. His right hand was on top of my folded hands and it looked as if I had one giant fist. Everybody was smiling and looked into the camera, except Hugo. His eyes were closed and he held his lips together tightly to hide his front tooth, broken in half two months earlier when a boy tripped him on the ice. Mom looked elegant with her left arm nonchalantly draped over her leg. You could see that her hair had thinned out. She worried that she would need to wear a wig someday. Her hair was like her dad's, who had been bald since his early thirties.

Mom was almost as tall as Dad, especially when she wore high heels. But Mom didn't like high heels. She liked to dress in a casual manner, preferring light wool vests that she wore loose and unbuttoned. Her dark skin tanned quickly without getting sunburned. She highlighted her beautiful tan by wearing white and light-colored dresses. When Mom rubbed me with suntan lotion she would tell me that I had her kind of skin.

The salon door opened. Mom was angry.
"You, *mispunt*! Can't you listen? Get out of the room!"
I became scared when she was mad: she'd purse her lips and her eyes became even darker.
"OK, OK, Mom. I'm going."
"August, this is our special room for entertaining guests. Don't play in here!"

The room meant a lot to her. But we never had guests.

2

Kindergarten Treats

My kindergarten school was on Gasthuis Street, just two blocks away from our house. After my first day, Mom told me that I was now ready to go to school by myself. I enjoyed the adventurous walk to school, catching the admiring glances of classmates who were dropped off by their mothers on bicycles.

Dominican nuns were in charge of the school. Supported by the local Catholic church, they owned a beautiful, large building. Before World War II, it had been the house of the local notary. The classrooms were filled with new toy cars, cranes, and light brown wooden blocks.

My teacher, Sister Silvester, wore a long, black nun's robe. Her wrinkled face was tightly wrapped in the black headdress. Sister was very strict about her students' bathroom breaks. A good reason was required to go outside the fixed daily timeframe.

"Sister Silvester, I need to go to the bathroom now."
"Are you sure, August?"
"Yes, Sister."
"We will all go in twenty minutes. Can you wait?"
I crossed my legs, trying to signal the urgency of my request.
Sister looked at me sternly, and paused.
"Be quick about it. We can't have you go whenever you want to," she finally said.
I raced out the door.

At the end of the first month, I celebrated my fifth birthday at school. Because the late September weather was still nice, Mom told me to wear my Sunday shorts. I hated shorts because they made me feel like a baby. I had quietly hoped for cold weather so I didn't have to wear them. Mom handed me a brown paper bag with treats: small fruit candies, wrapped in shiny red, green, and yellow paper.
"August, I will be going along with you to take pictures."
"That's neat, Mom."
"We'll go by bike. It's getting late," Mom said with a hurried voice. Sister Silvester did not like tardiness.

On the bike, I started to feel nervous. I did not like getting all the attention on my birthday. When we entered the school, I forgot to say hello to Sister, who smiled at Mom.
"So this is August's big day," she said.
"Yes. He has been talking about it all the time," Mom answered.
"Look, August, I have something for you."
Sister Silvester bent down and gave me a shiny yellow crown.
"Do you like it?"
"Yes, Sister Silvester," I whispered.
I carefully put it on my head, pushing the crown down so it wouldn't fall off.

When I entered the classroom, everybody was already on the floor in a circle.
"We're all here now. Let's start," Sister Silvester said.
"Lang zal hij leven, lang zal hij leven..."
Blushing, I tightly gripped the bag with treats.
"OK, August, hand out the treats now," Sister Silvester said.
I opened the bag and carefully held it in front of my classmates.
"Only one. Take only one," I said firmly, as I was moving around the circle. When we left home in the morning, Mom had told me that I should hand out only one piece of candy for each classmate. I heard the clicking of Mom's camera.

When I was done I had a lot of candies left in the bag and I realized that I could keep the leftovers for myself. I stopped handing out treats.

On birthdays, you were allowed to play with your favorite toys in the classroom. I had been dreaming about building a large fort. There were lots of wooden blocks in the room and I started working on them. Mom stayed for more pictures.

Within minutes, I had built a long wall of blocks. It was great not having to share the blocks. And I had my bag with leftover candy to eat at home.

Mom picked me up on her bicycle at the end of the day. On the way home she told me that we might move to another town.
"Why?" I asked.
"Well, August, our house needs a lot of repairs. We have big cracks in the front wall. It might be better for us to get a new house."
When we arrived home she pointed out some of the cracks running across the width of the brick front. I had never noticed them. Mom looked worried as she was staring at the wall.
"One day, this house is going to fall down. I know it," she mumbled.
"Why do we need to leave Tiel, Mom?" I asked.
"That has to do with Daddy's business, August."

3

Hugo's Bike

On his tenth birthday, my parents gave Hugo a new bike. It was dark blue with white, plastic grips on the handle bar. Hugo had been begging for a bike because most of his classmates had one. From that first day, he went everywhere by bike, even outside Tiel to towns like Zoelen and Kerk-Avezaath.

My Dad gave Hugo the bike so he could deliver photo packages around town. Hugo installed a two-sided bag on the back of the bike for the packages.

When he wasn't out delivering packages I'd go with him on rides, sitting in the back. I held the frame tightly, trying to keep my fingers out of the springs under Hugo's seat. If I moved my legs too much, the bags would hit the spokes of the wheel, setting off a whirring noise. If the bags got stuck in the wheel, they could cause bad crashes.

In the spring, Hugo took me for a ride to see the fruit orchards. It was warm already, with little wind. After leaving town, we smelled the manure at nearby farms.
"Hugo, this smells awful," I said.
"Yeah. It's pretty bad. Press down with your fingers on your nose. Like this."
He turned around to show me. He biked comfortably with only one hand on the handle bar.
"I can't breathe," I said with a stuffy voice.
"Just breathe through your mouth. It's easy."

It didn't feel comfortable but at least it didn't smell.
After a while, Hugo took his fingers off his nose.
"The coast is clear, August."
I started breathing through my nose again. He was right. We laughed.

The blossoms at Avezaath's cherry orchards smelled wonderful. A sea of pink-white flowers on the trees extended on our right. Every ten yards, the trees lined up straight, parallel to the narrow ditches separating the orchards, then the trees made diagonals until they were straight again for a short moment as we moved by. I loved the patterns whizzing by.
Beyond the cherry orchards were the apple and pear orchards. The trees were in bloom and the air was filled with the blossom's scent. We had forgotten the manure.

We came to the dike at the river. Hugo arched his back and stood on the pedals to climb the steep, narrow road up the dike. Midway, I got off because we had lost speed. I ran after Hugo who was now moving quickly without me. Tall grass grew on the sides of the dike and the wildflowers were blooming in yellow, purple, and white. A white butterfly flew around the wildflowers. I jumped onto the backseat again. It made the bike swerve but Hugo kept going. As we rode along the top of the dike, the wind picked up, and Hugo was working hard to move us along. Already, cows were grazing in the fertile *uiterwaard* between the summer and winter dikes. In the distance, the low water in the river was quietly hugging the summer dike.
"August, let's go home now. I'm getting tired," Hugo said quickly through his heavy breathing.
"OK, Hugo."

He took the first turn off the dike and we raced down, squinting our eyes in the draft wind.
"Hugo, can we avoid the manure?" I asked.
"I don't think so. There are farms everywhere."

4

Witness

It was Sunday morning. The little red alarm clock in the bedroom read seven o'clock. Hugo was still sound asleep in the other bed. I put my face close to his, listening to his quiet breathing, in and out, in and out. I went to the window where two sparrows had made themselves comfortable on the ledge. The sun was up, shining into the room.

A black car passed in the street below. I could hear the voices of my father and mother, arguing in the kitchen. I was curious and I tiptoed down the stairs to the hallway. Carefully, I stood close to the kitchen door, trying not to make a single sound. I heard my father open his tin can of tobacco. He always smoked cigarettes before breakfast. I was familiar with the sharp smell of his dark tobacco from the black and blue Van Nelle package.

"Charles, I am too tired. That's all," my mother said softly.
"But *Rineke*, what am I supposed to do? Without your help, I can't keep up in the summer season. You know that."
He continued, in a louder voice: "What do you want me to do? We can't afford outside help."
"Money. Always money. Isn't there anything else you can talk about?!"
Mom's voice sounded as if she was going to cry.

"Please *Rineke*, don't get upset. We'll try to find a way."
I could hear her cry. Slowly, I moved back up the stairs. Hugo should know about this. I woke him up and he looked at me sleepily when I told him my story.
"Don't worry, August. It's not a big deal. I'm going to go back to sleep." He turned his back to me, pulling the blanket over his head.
I stayed in bed looking at the ceiling. I was scared.
At breakfast, I noticed that Mom's eyes were red. She was silent and left the table early to go up to her bedroom.

Around noon, the doorbell rang. I raced to the front to open the door. There was Oma Brouwers, Mom's mother, still dressed for High Mass.
"Hello August, how are you today?" She looked serious.
"Fine, Oma."
Dad appeared at the bottom of the stairs.
"Hello, Charles." Oma said it quietly.
"Come in. I'll take your coat," Dad said.
Oma's arrival was an unexpected treat on a boring Sunday. She made tea and we ate cookies.
"August, why don't you go play somewhere. Oma and I need to talk now," Dad said.
I got up and left the kitchen.
In the hallway, I faintly heard Oma's voice.
"Where is she now?"
I played in the long hallway. The large granite tiles were great for sliding on your socks and I ran fast to make the long slides back and forth.
Oma and Dad left the kitchen, silently going up the stairs.
After a few minutes, I stopped sliding because a hole in my sock was slowing me down.

Suddenly, there were sounds upstairs. Mom stood at the top of the stairway, her arms up in the air. She was wearing her bathrobe. Her eyes were wide open, I had never seen them like that before. I was afraid that Mom would come down and hit me.
Oma was standing next to her.
"Riny, calm down, calm down!" she commanded. Oma tried grabbing Mom's arms, but they were flailing up and down uncontrollably. Mom was breathing in quick bursts as if she was out of breath.

I heard Dad coming down from the dark room. He quickly whisked Mom back into the bedroom.
It was silent again.
 Oma looked down at me from the top of the stairs. She looked even graver than before. Without a word she briskly turned away from me and went into my parents' bedroom.
I put on my shoes. I wanted to go outside.

5

Last Day At Hoogeinde

In early October we were getting ready to move to the new town, Culemborg. It was smaller than Tiel, about fifteen miles to the northwest, at the Lek river. Across the river, the large city of Utrecht was about 15 miles away. Mom and Dad had been packing for several weeks and the hallway of the House in Tiel was filled with large carton boxes, stacked up against the walls. I couldn't do my sock slides in the hallway anymore.

I decided to go for a last walk through Tiel. I put on my boots and coat and opened the front door. The October temperature was nice and a gentle breeze moved the scattered leaves on the trees. The sun occasionally peeked through the clouds. Last night's rain had left big puddles on the sidewalk. I made sure to get my boots right in the middle of the biggest one and splashed hard enough to get my pants wet. My mother told me to stay away from the puddles but I enjoyed the splashing so much.

I went down Hoogeinde street, past the *Middenstands* Bank which was managed by Mr. Michels, our neighbor. The Michels family lived upstairs from the Bank. The black wrought iron fencing on the front windows looked stately and the building stood out on our street because its bricks were a different color brown. Next to the Bank was the house with the large dark green door. The people that used to live there had just moved out. I played often with their son in the backyard. It had so many trees that you could easily get lost during our hide-and-seek games. I missed playing in that backyard. Our yard had no trees and was too small for hide-and-seek games. Instead of trees, we had ivy on the back wall in the summer.

     I turned to the right onto Lange Street. Mom and Dad didn't like it when I went there by myself because it was a busy street with narrow sidewalks. At one part the sidewalk was only one tile wide and you had to walk sideways to stay on. And you could easily bump into the large gray metal light poles. Hugo once walked into a pole and came home with a bloody nose. At first, Mom and Dad didn't understand what had happened.
"Hugo, why didn't you see the pole?" Mom asked.
"Well, I…"
Pause.
"Well, Hugo?"
"I was looking at the clouds. They looked neat," Hugo finally conceded.
"You daydreamer!"
My mother said it with a smile as she gave Hugo a handkerchief to stop the bleeding. I was always careful on Lange Street.
     I turned in front of the Gymnasium high school where students learned Latin and Greek. They were the sons and daughters of businessmen, doctors or notaries. Usually, several generations in one family had gone to this Gymnasium. Dad told me that his sisters went there.
"If you work hard in grade school you can go to the Gymnasium and study at the University," he said.
Dad talked about school often and told us how important it was. Hugo took advanced credit in junior high so he could go to a high school that qualified for University entrance. My father had big plans for us in school.
     St. Dominicus Catholic church was opposite from the Gymnasium in Tiel. The church was entirely made of brick in various shades of brown. Inside, the curved lines of brick met at the top of the high ceiling and I felt dizzy looking all the way up. St. Dominicus was the new Catholic church. A mile down the road was St. Maarten, the old Catholic church. During the Reformation it had become the Protestant church. St. Maarten was larger than our church and Dad told me that it was more beautiful. There were no statues or pictures in the church: the

Protestants had taken all of them out. I had never been inside. I wasn't supposed to go into a Protestant church.

We never went to church together. My father stayed home. He prayed at our meals but he did not want to be in church on Sundays. I had the feeling that he was afraid to go out and meet people.

The election was one of the few times that Dad went out because every Dutch citizen was required to vote. Since his first vote in the 1930's Dad faithfully voted KVP, the Roman Catholic party, a standard vote for Catholics since the 19th Century, encouraged by the Catholic Church. Hugo laughed about it because he thought it was old-fashioned.

Even outside of the Season, if Dad was very busy, Mom often ended up helping him out by drying and sorting pictures. When she couldn't go to church with us, Hugo and I went with Oma Brouwers and our aunts, Netty and Fie. Opa Brouwers never went with us. He didn't really believe in God, Oma once whispered to me. Otherwise he would be in church, she added.

I enjoyed going to church with Oma. She wore her Sunday hat with a small feather and she dressed in her finest clothes. Taking her customary seat in church she carefully looked around, often bending over to whisper comments to one of my aunts. They were busy because the High Mass was crowded and they knew a lot of people. A good reason to come to High Mass was the opportunity to see many people.

"Did you see Mrs. Gerritsen? I haven't seen her in church for weeks," Oma said to Aunt Netty.

"I heard she's been ill. She was in the hospital for a while," Aunt Netty whispered to Oma, who continued to carefully look at people entering the church.

"She still looks a bit pale, don't you think?" Oma inquired.

Aunt Netty nodded seriously.

"Oh, look at Mrs. De Vries!" Aunt Fie said.

Oma and Aunt Netty turned their heads in unison.

"It doesn't look good on her. I liked it better when she had curls," Oma commented.

"It's just awful," Aunt Netty said, half-loud.

They nodded together.

Oma and my aunts were very social about their church visits. After Mass, I would joke about their gossiping and imitated the way they looked around and talked about people's hats and hairdos. They loved my imitations and we laughed a lot.

The road went slightly upward near the canal where the butcher's store overlooked the water. The floor was covered in shiny, glazed tiles so that the butcher could easily clean up the blood that dripped from the cutting boards. The pungent smell of raw meat hit me when I passed the front door. On the sidewall somebody has written the letters "O.A.S." in white paint. I had asked Dad about the letters when I got home.
"The OAS are bad men in Algeria who kill innocent people," he said.
"Where's Algeria?"
"In Africa, August."
"Why do they kill people, Dad?"
"It's hard to explain. It's political."
I didn't understand the last word.
"Who is writing that name on the wall?"
"Just people who want to show off. Don't worry about it, August."

As I continued on my walk through Tiel on that last day before we moved, I crossed the bridge over the canal. It had stone walls on both sides and a long green metal bar ran along the top of each wall. I could just reach the bar with my hand if I stood on my toes. At the end of the bar was a sharp point, that curved up. I loved touching it.

The neighborhood across the canal was poor. It had several houses with black-and-white 'Uninhabitable' signs. The windows were shut with wooden panels and broken pieces of gutter hung from the roofs. The fresh garbage outside was proof that people lived in these houses. My parents said that it was ridiculous that government couldn't do something about it.
Hoping that nobody would come out of the front doors of these houses, I always ran past them toward the end of the canal.

At the end of the canal, St. Maarten Church rose above the trees. Opa Brouwers, Mom's father, took me for walks along the canal past the church tower. The street was lined with large oak trees, and a heavily wooded park stretched on the city side of St. Maarten. Before World War II, St. Maarten had the tallest tower between the Waal and Lek rivers. Opa told me that on a clear day people could see more than thirty miles from the

top of the tower, all the way to the Dom Cathedral Tower in Utrecht. But now, St. Maarten Tower was still in ruins from the bombing during the war. Half of the tower was gone. One day, as I was walking past the tower with Opa, I asked him who had done that to the tower.
"The Germans did it. They bombed it in the war."
"Naughty men, the Germans," I said.
He smiled at me, nodding his head.
 When I was older Opa told me that the Americans had in fact bombed St. Maarten because the Germans had used the tower to follow Allied troop movements south of the river in September 1944.

 Opposite St. Maarten's was Tiel's indoor swimming pool. Hugo went there often. The blue-green water had a strong taste of chlorine and I hated the deep water. I wanted to be able to stand when I was swimming. My brother always laughed when I said that.
 As I continued toward the river dike, the Bleach Field was on my left. The annual Fair in Tiel was held at the Bleach Field in early fall. On Wednesday, large trucks arrived to unload equipment. Long wooden beams were laid out across the grounds and crews spent Thursday and Friday to get the rides ready. The Fair started on Friday night. With songs of Elvis, Little Richard, and Sam the Sham blaring in the background, almost everyone in Tiel came to the Field to enjoy the rides, eat pancakes and candy, and drink Coca-Cola and beer. I loved the "Always Prize" attractions, especially the tent with the red wooden fish in the water tank. Using a small net I caught the fish and looked for the number on the inside. Number two was the big prize: the plastic Indian set with the bow and arrow. The arrows had light-brown rubber tops and the bow worked well because the arrows went far. Hugo took the CakeWalk ride with its moving steps and stairs. I admired him for getting onto that ride. The Caterpillar ride went up and down in a circle and in the middle of the ride a long curtain went over the top of the carts. Hugo convinced me to go on it. The speed of the ride made me feel dizzy and I panicked after the curtain went down. I screamed as hard as I could and they stopped the ride. Relieved, I got out. Hugo was embarrassed. On the way back to Oma I was trembling.

The clouds were moving fast in the wind, in front of the sun and away again, sending sharp, blinding rays on the wet bricks. A group of children was walking across the Bleach Field. I recognized Peter, a tall blonde boy, who acted as the group's leader. They were Protestants, and sometimes we fought with them. They went to their own school across town. There was a stubborn rivalry between the Protestants and the Catholics. After our fights, we had scratches, bloody noses and torn clothes. I wondered if Catholics and Protestants would fight in my new town. The Protestant kids looked at me. I would have to run if they went after me. To my relief they turned away, toward downtown Tiel.

I hurried down the street that led to the cut in the dike. Already, I could hear the steady murmur of the boats' engines. I loved running up the dike after the rain had made the grass soggy, slipping several times before reaching the top, with mud and grass on my pants. From the dike, I squinted to see the long, flat Rhine boats on the Waal river. Laundry was waving on the decks and some boats had a small car on board. Bobbing in the waves, a small *parlevink* boat was selling supplies to one of the boats. Across the river, at the town of Wamel, the car ferry was making its stop. I could see cars driving off the ferry and people were tiny dots as they rode their bicycles off the ferry.

The Waal river was wide at Tiel and its current very strong. Powerful squalls close to the piers could drown inexperienced swimmers in seconds. When she was in her teens Mom swam across the Waal several times. She mentioned to us how tired she was when she finally reached the beach at Wamel, and that she needed to rest for a long time, lying on the sand. It made me proud that she had made the crossings because I didn't know any other moms who had done this. I knew that Dad was also proud because he mentioned Mom's swimming feats regularly. Hugo could do it someday, I thought, but I knew I wasn't a candidate. The water was too deep for me. I couldn't stand in it.

Two large black gas reservoirs rose behind The Waal Cafe, a pretty, white brick building on the dike, with a small terrace facing the river. The bar opened early in the morning and many bikes were lined up near the front door.
"These people are the worst," my father told me once. "They drink their lives away, these do-nothings!" I was curious what

they looked like. Quickly, I glanced inside as I was walking past the open front door. It was hard to see people through the thick smoke of tobacco. The bar was filled with people who had small glasses in front of them. It was quiet inside, the only sound I heard was the ticking of billiard balls.

I turned left to go up to the ancient brick city walls. They protect downtown Tiel against the flooding of the Waal river. Dad loved to tell us about the 1926 flood. He was eleven years old and the water was only ten inches from the top of the walls. At the downtown pharmacy, officials had posted a daily sign to show the rise or fall of the water of the Rhine river at Cologne, Germany. Every day after school, Dad went there to see the sign. One day, it read "Cologne, rise, 1/2 inch" and another "Cologne, rise, 1/4 inch." Day after day, the sign said "rise." Standing on the city walls, Dad could touch the water with his hands. Trees in front of the walls had vanished under water and looking across, toward the town of Wamel, there was a vast lake covering the *uiterwaard* areas between summer and winter dikes. It looked beautiful and scary at the same time.

Several days later, with the water less than four inches from the top of the walls, the pharmacy sign read "Cologne, fall, 1/4 inch." The water was receding. Tiel was safe. Dad ran home and proudly told his parents the good news. I liked Dad's story. Floodings sounded exciting.

From the top of the walls I overlooked the Kaai, the large grass field that bordered the river. The Kaai flooded easily, turning the field into a gigantic puddle. In the fall the grass was wet and we returned home with muddy clothes after a game of soccer. Last summer at the Kaai, Hugo won first prize in running and the long jump in the City championships. He had beaten his cousin Frank, one of Uncle Louis' sons, in the running finals. Although Frank was faster Hugo had won because he outsmarted Frank at the turning point. Instead of going all around the tree, as Frank did, Hugo merely touched the front of the tree before racing back. Frank was livid but apparently nobody had said that you needed to go around the tree. Hugo received two black-and-yellow ribbons with silver letters. The same night, he put them on the wall next to his bed.

Every year, the circus set up its big tent at the Kaai. Hugo and I wasted no time to see the wild animals. I loved the tiger. He was beautiful with his yellow-and-black stripes, pacing back and forth quickly in the small travel cage. I was never able to laugh much at the clowns because I thought they were exaggerating. But I loved the animals: the horses, elephants, tigers and lions.

I jumped off the short end of the city wall and crossed the street to the harbor. Tiel's harbor was small. Most boats were in transit to Rotterdam or to the Ruhr area in Germany. Whenever a new boat docked, I tried to get close to see what was on the deck. I often saw toys I had never seen before. It would be neat to travel on the water and see new places, I thought. The mom was at work on deck, taking off laundry from the long clothesline. I wondered how the children went to school.

Watching the loading and unloading of the boats was fun. The cargo space opened as long cover panels turned outward and the scoops from harbor cranes lifted sand or river pebbles from the boat, dropping their loads onto tall hills at the quay.

It was a thrill to climb the pebble and sand hills on the waterfront but my parents warned me to stay away from them. Dad once told me about a boy who suffocated when a mountain of sand started to move and buried him. But nothing ever happened to me. The large pebble hills were tough to climb. My feet would sink deep into the white and gray pebbles and I had to keep moving quickly to avoid getting stuck. On the top of the hill I had beautiful view of the harbor and I counted the ships docked at the harbor. Today there were six. The sun was high, coming out of the clouds. I needed to go back home for lunch. I would miss the harbor.

The narrow alley opened onto Fish Market Square. The alley was under repair and I dodged loose bricks. The Square was long and narrow, bordered by stately white houses. At the end of the square was a small podium with a marble table where the fish used to be auctioned. It still smelled of fish.

The podium connected to Pig Market Square, with its expensive sporting goods store. I often admired the leather balls in the window but Dad considered a leather soccer ball a luxury. Across from the store was China Garden, the new Chinese-Indonesian restaurant. Aunt Fie and Aunt Netty had already gone there for dinner.

Uncle Louis' photography store in the Voorstad bordered Pig Market Square. I waited in the store until Uncle Louis was finished with a customer in his studio. The studio was behind the store, separated by a curtain, and I could hear my uncle talking to the customer.
"Please look a little more to the left. Yes, that's good."
Click. "Look at my hand. Yes, right."
Click, click.
With every click a photo flash cut through the open top of the heavy red curtain. Uncle Louis smiled at me when he opened the curtain. He wore thick glasses with a modern, dark frame and, unlike Dad, he still had most of his hair. My uncle didn't look like Dad and he was more upbeat and talkative.
"Just give me a minute. I am almost done."
The customer ordered his pictures.
"You can pick them up the day after tomorrow," Uncle Louis said.
"Thank you. Goodbye."
The door bell rang as the customer left.
"Can I see the studio?" I asked.
"Of course. Go ahead, but don't touch any of the camera equipment," he warned.
Uncle Louis opened the curtain and I went into the studio. It had several big spotlights and fancy cameras on tripods with flashlights. My uncle remained in the store while I tried every chair in the studio, pretending to pose for pictures. A few minutes later my uncle returned, sticking his head through the curtain.
"I have to leave now. I have a wedding to do," he said.
"You can stay if you want. My assistant will be in the store now," Uncle Louis continued.
I quickly got off the chair.
"No, I better go. It's time for lunch," I said.
"See you later, August."
"Bye."
Uncle Louis was at home in his store, meeting customers and explaining the newest camera designs. He would be pushing up his sagging glasses with a quick routine move. Moving around his studio in a nonchalant and easy way, he was always very concentrated behind the camera. You could sense his eagerness to get the right shot and he instantly knew when he had it, telling the customer that he was done. I never saw Dad like that. It took him thirty minutes to set up the tripod

correctly, make lighting measurements and get the background right. For a single picture he could take over three minutes. It was too long for me to pose naturally. Dad acted as if each picture was carved out of pure gold.
"August, don't you realize how expensive it is to develop a roll?" he said.
"No, Dad. But I bet you do."
"I am not going to waste any of these pictures, do you understand?"

Dad's pictures were stiff and stilted. His perfectionism drove him to do it just the right way while he was unaware of the people around him. As a photographer, he would add an hour to any wedding reception. Dad was more at home in the dark room.

I turned onto Water Street where Campagne's Photography store was just around the corner. Campagne was Uncle Louis' major competitor in town. His window display looked better than my uncle's and the inside of the store was modern. Dad told me that Uncle Louis earned his money mostly with wedding pictures because he was the town's best photographer at receptions.

I went down Water Street past Vroom and Dreesmann, Tiel's big department store. After school, I loved to roam in the store. My favorite place was the toy department on the second floor. I could try out all the toys I wanted. Sometimes, classmates were there too and we played soccer in the aisles with plastic balls.

Next to Vroom and Dreesmann is De Gruyter's grocery store where Mom did her shopping. At the back wall of the store, on shiny yellow tiles, was a painting of Indonesian women working the rice fields. It must have been from the time that Indonesia was still a colony of The Netherlands.

I ran faster, passing the Hendrich Gramophone Store in the middle of Water Street. Gerard Hendrich, the owner's son, was my best friend. Gerard and I had been friends together since we were three years old. He was thin and much taller than me. He was always in a good mood, ready to explore the town with me.

We loved playing on the mountains of rubble left by crews demolishing war-torn houses. We jumped on slabs of concrete, balancing our weights if the slabs started to move. We climbed up the larger slabs, jumping into the rubble, and coughing hard because of the dust. We scraped our toes when our sandals got stuck on the armored wire sticking out from the slabs. Wearing shorts, our legs turned white from the dust of the concrete.

Construction crews moved in after the rubble was removed and quickly built many series of straight, modern houses. Gerard and I made many trips through town but it was getting hard to find rubble mountains, even at the outskirts of town. After dark, we liked to run through Plantsoen Park with our heads held up, and pretended that the stars were going by.

At the Hoogeinde home, Gerard and I played a lot with the water faucets. One day, we turned on the water in the kitchen and went upstairs to play in my bedroom. Half an hour later Mom called from downstairs. The kitchen and the hallway were flooded.

"August, can you please be more careful next time. This is a mess!"

"Yes, Mom. I will," I said sheepishly.

"Go outside now while I clean this up."

Gerard and I left as fast as we could.

Outside, Gerard told me that my mom was very nice to us about the flooding. He was right. Sometimes Mom could get mad very quickly but other times she would be quiet. Maybe she was nice because Gerard was visiting.

When I visited Gerard's home, above the gramophone store, usually at least one of his brothers was playing music. Frits, the oldest, played the piano, Thieu played the trumpet, while Gerard and Henk played the drums. Mrs. Hendrich would bring cookies into the large living room while I read my favorite Tin-Tin cartoons. Mrs. Hendrich once told me that she was in Dad's class in high school. I wondered what that was like but I didn't ask her. I always ate the cookies instead.

I passed Waltman's bakery at the corner of Water Street and Hoogeinde. Wonderful pies and pastries filled the window. Dad claimed they were overpriced. Every day, Hugo and I went to Waltman to buy fresh bread. We asked for half a white and half a brown bread, uncut. If we didn't have cash we had the amount "written down" for payment next time. On the way home, I ate pieces of the freshly baked bread by digging my fingers into the warm bread.

"Have the mice been eating from this, or is it you?" Dad would ask.
"I think it's the mice," I'd say and looked the other way.
He wouldn't respond.
I liked it that he let me get away with it.

     I crossed the street, walking toward the post office. There was a brass panel with the face of a former postal director. He had been executed in the war.
In the small alley at the back end of the post office, Ome Roelof, our neighbor, was leading his horse to the cart with the brightly painted red and green wheels. Ome Roelof moved to Tiel from his farm near Avezaath but he kept his horse and cart for large loads such as coal or bricks.
I loved to touch the large horse on the side of his head.
"Be careful. He is not in a great mood today," warned Ome Roelof.
I stepped back as the horse breathed heavily and shook his head.
"I am going home for lunch now, Ome Roelof!"
"See you."

     My boots and pants were muddy and I felt hungry and tired. I rang our doorbell.
"August, lunch is ready. Come in quickly," Mom said hurriedly.
"Where have you been? You are so dirty!" she continued.
I took off my boots.
"Mom, do we need to move? I like it here."

6

The New Town

Our new house in Culemborg was nicer than Hoogeinde 5. We now ate in the dining room instead of the kitchen. We did not have a dining room at Hoogeinde. My parents liked our new bathroom with the large bathtub and Dad was happy that he didn't have to bother with metal tubs anymore. He built a dark room in the attic and had enough room left to set up his train track. We had a garage with a long driveway next to the house. It was made of long pink stone tiles and Hugo and I played hop, skip and jump in the driveway. It was easy to find out how far we went because the tiles were one meter long.

The living room was heated with a coal furnace. In October, the coal man arrived to deliver the first batch of coal for the winter. He drove a flatbed truck, blackened by coal dust and filled with large hemp coal bags. He would pick up a bag from his truck and, bending his body forward to balance the weight, sling the top of the sack over his head. His face and hands were shiny black from handling the anthracite coal. He emptied the bag in our wooden coal box in the garage.

We used a coal bucket to get coal from the garage for the furnace. The shiny black bucket was two and a half feet tall with one end at the top shaped like a scoop. I didn't have to fetch coal from the garage because the filled bucket was too heavy for me.

The coal furnace in the living room had small windows made from transparent mica. You could press your finger against it and the mica would move a little.
Dad became angry when he saw me play with the mica.
"August, if you break one of these we can't use the furnace anymore! The mica is very expensive." I couldn't understand that we would need to get a new furnace if the mica broke.
I would stop touching the mica until Dad left the room. Then I'd start playing again. When the sunlight caught the mica it reflected the colors of the rainbow. It looked beautiful.
In the morning, my task was to empty the ash can in the furnace. I would move a handle at the bottom of the furnace back and forth. The handle opened a trap door and the burnt coals would drop into the can. If I moved the handle too much, hot coals started falling into the can. Then the ashes would get too hot to throw them out and I'd have to wait to clean up the ashes.

The bottom drawer of the bookcase in the living room was filled with Dinky Toys, Lego, and plastic soldiers. After emptying the drawer, I could spend hours sorting the toys. When I was done, I threw all of it back for more sorting next time.

On Sunday afternoons Dad worked on his train track upstairs. He was always busy rewiring and setting up new pieces. I was allowed to play with the trains after he was done. By moving a white plastic dial on the small green transformer the train started moving. It took more than a minute before it rounded the full track. After a while I tried to go at maximum speed but the train would derail in a curve and Dad had to go under the tracks to reset the train. Dad built small luggage packages for the train station by gluing matches and he painted a sequence of oil paintings for the background. He used the church in Avezaath as one of his models. Avezaath's white church tower had become very familiar to me. Dad also built a portable version of the track that could be stored in a large wooden suitcase. The wooden letters on the suitcase said: "The Hugo and August Railway System." We never took it anywhere because it was too heavy to carry unless you went by car. And we didn't have a car.
In the winter, when business was slow, Dad would spend hours at night doodling with his model train set. Hugo and I never went upstairs because he didn't want us to play while he

was working on the trains. He strictly reserved our play time for Sundays only.

Dad didn't like most board games and Mom was often too absent-minded to play. Hugo was the only one who played games with me. I loved soccer and I had a big collection of soccer games. My favorite game was one that I had made up. The playing field was Mom's large serving board. I had made soccer goals from electrical wire, with first aid gauze for nets. The ball was a piece of aluminum foil that I made as round as possible by rolling it in my hands; the teams were buttons I had found in Mom's sewing drawer. I usually managed to find enough to get two teams of eleven players with matching colors.

I played the quarterfinals with Dad; he was easy to beat because he was not interested. He never remembered my rules although they were not difficult. The semifinals were against Mom. Occasionally, she was interested enough to play a little but I would always end up winning my games with her. In the final game I played Hugo. He was a tough player but I always won by one goal. Sometimes I wondered why I always won by one goal.

As in Tiel, the salon room was off limits to Hugo and me. Shortly after our move, my parents bought a piano for the salon. The upright piano was light brown. The day after it arrived, I slipped into the salon. The piano was in the corner, next to the bay window. I opened the keyboard cover and the morning sunlight reflected on the black and white keys. I loved the shiny keys. Carefully, I tried the keys. It didn't sound the way my father played. How did he do it?

My parents heard me play and admonished me for being in the salon. But at the next opportunity I would try again to make music like Dad's.

Dad played the piano on Sunday afternoons. It was easy to see and hear him in the living room because the rooms were separated only by glass sliding doors. He would lean back, lift his chin, and start playing. He always did a lot of cross-overs with his hands. He looked serious when he played and the sounds of his music were solemn. I liked his music, it flowed nicely. He sometimes played for more than an hour without any written music, improvising the whole time.

Dad told me that Grandpa Swanenberg would visit the opera and afterwards sat down at the piano at home to play the tunes he had heard that night from memory. To me, it sounded like magic. And I could tell that Dad was also in awe of Grandpa.

    In the first months after we moved Dad took a liking to our neighbors, the Mandos family. Mr. Mandos was a tall man. He sold insurance. His hair was always combed straight back, oddly highlighting his baldness in front. Mrs. Mandos was talkative and friendly, but became quiet when it came to serious topics, always deferring to her husband. They were younger than my parents. Mr. Mandos bought a car several weeks after we moved in: a gray Wartburg from East Germany. It was the only one in town. The car made strange noises, almost like a small motorcycle. Kids at school laughed when I told them about the car. They said that the car had only two cylinders.
    Dad liked the Mandos family so much, we even visited with them. Our house was part of a duplex so the Mandos family were our only immediate neighbors. I often played with the two Mandos children, Paul and Marion, who were about my age. After a few months,, though, my father became angry with the Mandos family. He believed that the children were following him through their house and were jumping down the stairs to tease him, making noises and screaming out loud. Hugo and I would get tense when we heard somebody jump down the stairs next door.
"They follow me through the house," Dad said angrily.
"Oh, Dad, do you really believe that?!"
"They come down the stairs when I do. They follow me!"
"They're just running around. No big deal."
He shook his head. He just didn't believe us.
We did not visit the Mandos house anymore.

    Across the driveway, our neighbors were two old people, the Den Hartogs, who maintained a patch of farmland just outside town where they kept one cow. I exchanged hellos with Mrs. Den Hartog on my way to school, but the old man was grumpy and did not say much back, except for a unintelligible grumbling. He was small, and had a severely hunched back. On some days, the old lady treated Hugo and me to cookies and milk. Her cookies were good but the heated milk was straight from their cow and tasted funny. We noticed the skin on the milk and we waited for Mrs. Den Hartog to leave the room. Then we took the skin off and dropped it behind her dresser.

After the milk cooled down we drank it quickly, before a new skin formed.

One day in summer, I arrived home from school and noticed bikes parked in our driveway. When I walked into the living room, several boys from our street were inside. I recognized them but I had never played with them before.

Our TV had arrived. It was a Philips television with a dark wood cover. When the TV was off, the screen was light green. Everybody was very quiet, attentively watching a German police movie. We had never had so many people in our living room before. Even Dad had come down from the dark room and was watching with the group. He commented on the brightness and the sharpness of the picture. He was happy with his purchase. Mom brought in cookies for everybody. It was a celebration, the only one we ever had with kids from the neighborhood.

The purple and white lilac trees were in full bloom. I touched a flower with my nose and, inhaling deeply, smelled its fragrance. I had asked my parents for more lilac trees.
Mom often sat on the terrace overlooking the backyard. She enjoyed the sun, sitting in her white wicker chair. She looked thin in her summer dress. Dad warned us to let Mom alone and to not bother her. That was difficult for me. I wanted her to help me catch ants.
"Not now, August." She said it with a smile but she sounded determined.
I walked away to catch ants by myself.

The Westersingel canal stretched for two miles along the western part of Culemborg. Near the end of the Prijssestraat, the Singel canal ran from the Gispen metal furniture plant, the largest factory in town, to the northern part of town, near the train bridge over the Lek river. Our house was close to a curve with nice-looking houses. Closer to the river, past the soccer field, the houses became small, built in long, anonymous rows.

When the water in the canal was low, pieces of wood, bikes, and tree branches became visible and the sides of the canal became lined with dark gray mud. If the water stayed low for several days, rats would appear. Walking along the canal I could see the brown animals scurry in the mud under the small

houses across from our house. My mother was very alarmed when she saw it for the first time.
"Charles, look at that. They are hideous!" she would exclaim.
"Riny, don't worry. The City is going to demolish these houses. You won't see any rats after that."
"How can you be sure about that?" Mom said, unconvinced.
"They'll run out of food and move on to another part of the river."
"I bet it's going to be our house next," Mom said nervously.
"Don't worry. They'll be gone soon."
Dad was right. The houses were demolished within six months. We never saw a rat again.

On my way to school I went up the bridge across the canal. The fire house sat at the top of the bridge. When its garage doors were open I could see the big red trucks lined up. My friend Eddy's father was a volunteer fireman and he had shown us the inside of the trucks. Once, he put me in the front seat and I held the white steering wheel. I was so high up that it felt like standing on a ladder. I tried to touch the dashboard but it was too far for me. Eddy's dad smiled when he saw me move around in the seat.
"Are you ready to drive?" he asked.
"No. It's too big," I said, embarrassed.
"Wait until you try to move the steering wheel..."
I couldn't even imagine.
"Time to get out, August."
He helped me down.
I was about the size of the truck's front tire, I noticed.

Halfway on my way to school, I would walk along Culemborg's main street, the Zand Street. I glanced at the large cheeses displayed in Van Maanen's dairy store, and I jumped on the creaky wooden planks of the café's empty porch terrace. Next door, the Merckx pharmacy was advertising the newest creams and pills, and I quickly glanced at the chocolate pies in the window of the bakery store. The blacksmith's shop was located at a bend in the road, across from the school. The blacksmith kept his business going because of the large number of small farms in the Culemborg area. The shop was filled with farm tools, horseshoes, and large metal pieces, arranged around the large anvil. A fire always burned in the back. The noise of the big hammer slamming on the anvil woke me up as I walked by in the morning.

Sometimes, a farmer in wooden shoes was holding his horse outside the shop. The blacksmith, sitting on a tiny three-legged chair, was putting shoes on the horse. White smoke sizzled from the horse's foot when the hot iron shoe was fitted and the pungent smell of burnt flesh made me feel sick. The horse nervously moved but the blacksmith was strong and simply held on to the horse's leg, hammering in the shoe. He kept the metal nails in his mouth so his hands were free. He was amazing.

School was not much different in Culemborg; the building was about the same size and I was getting used to being called "the newcomer from Tiel." I liked the walk from Catholic school to our gym class at the public school building across the street.

In the hallway of the public school was a large color picture of the Vikings destroying Dorestad, an ancient town, now in ruins, near Tiel. In awe, I stared at the Viking who was lifting his sword in triumph while the town was burning in the background. He was tall with a long blond mustache that reached below his chin. I imagined the fear of Dorestad's people when they saw Viking ships coming down the river. A large picture of Saint Boniface was next to the Viking picture. He had converted the northern part of Holland to Christianity. It was not as lively as the Viking picture but I was fascinated by the saint's ancient dress. It looked as if he lived a long time ago. I wondered why we didn't have color pictures in our school. The only small painting we had was of a sailor in a dark slicker coat who was smoking a pipe. My teacher told me that his name was Brandaris.

"He was a hero, who risked his life to save people at sea," my teacher said.

I often looked at his face when I came down the stairs at school. He didn't look like a hero to me.

Every week, on Wednesdays, my class walked the four blocks from school to the St. Barbara Church for Mass. Just two years before, they had stopped the daily school Masses. The older kids talked about daily Mass with horror in their voices.

Once a month, we had Confession. Four priests were on duty to take Confession and we could choose the one we liked best. I preferred Father Stricker who was popular because he asked for only one Our Father and three Hail Mary's. No matter what you confessed to.

The pew next to Father Stricker's Confession booth was filled to capacity after the students had made their choice. The other priests were not as busy. While awaiting my turn, I thought hard about my sins. Father Stricker worked fast and I needed to come up with something quickly. I couldn't be in the booth without anything to say. I pressed the insides of my knees together. The usual sins raced through my mind: stealing cookies and sugar, teasing my brother, and not listening to my parents. Meanwhile, the teacher was keeping a close eye on us to make sure we were quiet. When it was my turn I stepped into the small booth. It smelled like humid, old wood. Behind the black wire-mesh window I saw the outline of the priest's face. His calm, soothing voice welcomed me and I would have preferred to listen to him instead of talking about my sins. After some urging by Father Stricker, I said:
"I fought with my brother and I took cookies out of the jar without asking."
"Were you mean to your brother when you fought?"
"I hit him hard on the nose and then I ran away," I said in a serious tone.
It had happened five months ago, and I had confessed it twice already. I felt bad that I couldn't come up with something better.
"Did you mean to hurt him or was it an accident?" Father Stricker probed. He looked up. I could see the reflection of purple on his robe.
"I didn't want to hurt him," I said quickly.
"Say one Our Father and three Hail Mary's," Father Stricker intoned quietly.
"Yes, Father. I will."

It was over too quickly because I liked Father Stricker's voice so much. I walked to the other side of the bench to join those who finished Confession. I knelt down to say my prayers. It felt good to pray right after confessing. I didn't pray this hard at home.

Mom didn't go to church on Sunday anymore. Hugo asked her about it but she didn't say much. Hugo and I started going to Mass together. Always joking during Mass, Hugo

whispered funny comments in my ears. When I started to laugh he looked ahead with a straight face as if nothing had happened. Then I laughed even harder. One time, during Consecration, he told me that the bells sounded like the bells for the last round in a track and field race. I laughed so hard that I had to leave Mass before Communion. It didn't count as a Mass visit, and I had to go later that day to make up.
I didn't understand how Hugo could keep a straight face while he was fooling around. I looked forward to going to Mass with him but I was never sure if I could make it through.

    For my First Communion, Mom took me to the clothing stores several times to make sure I had the right pair of pants. I didn't need to buy a shirt for the occasion because I already owned formal shirts that I wore with jackets every Sunday.
Mom was surprised that I liked wearing them.
"Most kids your age hate wearing jackets!" she said.
"I like it, Mom. It makes me feel like a grownup and I can put all kinds of things in my pockets."
"Try these pants. They should fit."
After trying on many pants, Mom finally found one she liked. I didn't like them but I knew they would be my Sunday pants and I would only have to wear them on special occasions.
    It was special going shopping with Mom. She promised that she would be at Communion Mass. I wanted her promise because she had missed several Sunday Masses recently. I did not think it was because of the work in the business because Dad had been watching lots of TV in the last few weeks.
    The sun was shining on the day of First Communion. I was happy to see Mom in church when we paraded down the aisle. She smiled proudly at me when I walked by her pew. She was sitting far back, in one of the last pews. The priest put the host on my tongue. The taste was a disappointment. It was like the edible paper we used in the kitchen when Hugo and I played fake Communion, carefully cutting out circles with a pair of scissors. The real host was stickier and it took an Our Father and a Hail Mary to finally get it off the roof of my mouth. I wondered if that was the amount of praying I was supposed to do.
After Mass, Mom treated Hugo and me to ice cream.
"Dad is working. He couldn't be here today," she said.
Hugo and I looked at each other for a split second. We didn't believe her. He never went to Mass.

My parents gave me a children's prayer book as the Communion gift. In meticulous handwriting, Hugo wrote a special message in the front of the book, commemorating my First Communion.

Mom started to complain about feeling tired even when she was not helping Dad in the business and she saw her doctor about it. She also had trouble sleeping. The doctor gave her sleeping pills but I still heard a lot of walking around at night. Dad was nervous, smoking more cigarettes than before. He was constantly rolling new cigarettes using his small mats. When I came home from school the first thing I noticed was the tobacco smell, now even stronger than in Tiel.
Dad began to talk about going on vacation.
"It's time we went somewhere with the whole family," he declared in a hopeful voice during lunch.
Hugo and I stopped eating.
"Where are we going?" we asked.
"Oh, somewhere near a forest."
"In Holland?" I asked impatiently.
"Yes, in Holland. We won't go too far."
One reason we wouldn't go far was that we didn't have a car. Dad was just making conversation. I didn't believe we would go on a vacation together. We didn't even go to church together. "Yeah, maybe we could go to Geldermalsen, that's within 10 miles. We could walk," I said in a slow, sarcastic tone.
Dad looked away.
"Oh August, come on," Hugo said.
Mom was quiet. She continued to eat.
"Well, when are we leaving ?" I insisted.
"We'll see, August, we'll see," Dad whispered.
"Sure!"
I threw my knife and fork on the plate as hard as I could. Then I got up and stomped out of the room. I went to my bedroom, lying face down on the bed, crying.

Dad was not working for Uncle Louis' business anymore. He had two new main clients, photo stores in Dordrecht and Breda. They chose Dad's business because he delivered high quality pictures, manually developed and finished. Most stores were now offering machine-developed pictures from large photo-processing plants. Dad was worried about the factories. The price for development was going down rapidly and people were starting to use color film. Dad only did black and white film. His equipment couldn't develop color film. He was more intense than ever about getting his packages out in time because the turnaround of the factories was much faster. He was proud about the superior quality of his work but he realized it would be a matter of time before he would be out of business.

I didn't go to camp anymore. Mom said that she did not mind having me around and Dad had said that I was old enough to help at home. I loved staying home in the summer.
Every day, Hugo took the packages for Dordrecht and Breda to the post office. The post office closed at 6:00 p.m. and my father scrambled almost every day to get the packages finished on time. They were about the size of a small shoebox, made out of light brown packaging paper and tied together with thin rope. Dad was an expert at putting them together. After he was done he would hand the packages to Hugo who normally had about ten minutes to get to the post office before it closed. It was the end of Dad's day and he relaxed by smoking a cigarette while Hugo took off.

Sometimes I joined Hugo on his bike for the ride to the post office. He could really fly on his bike, even with me sitting in the back. He raced past the old windmill without the sails, down the street that connected to the Binnenpoort. I was excited when he raced down the street at high speed. Hugo turned left at the Kramer Freher toy store and through the Binnenpoort. The road inside the Binnenpoort was narrow and we bumped into pedestrians on the sidewalk when a car passed us. The Binnenpoort lead into Culemborg's Market Square. St. Barbara Church was on our right. Several older people, early for evening Mass, were walking up the church stairs. We crossed the market square to get to the post office. Hugo braked suddenly, just in front of the entrance to the post office. I could hear him breathing hard because of his fast ride. He walked in and said hello to the clerks. They knew him well because he was there every day, rain or shine. He took a receipt for the postage costs because Dad kept close track of costs and always asked Hugo for the receipt.

On the way back, Hugo was no longer in a hurry. Dad had asked him to buy eggs and cheese and he stopped at the cheese store. We bought 10 eggs and a pound of cheese. I was hugging the bike frame tightly with my legs, holding the cheese

and the egg carton. We were on our way home. At the old windmill without the sails Hugo stopped and asked me for the eggs. Without saying a word, he took out an egg and threw it as hard as he could against the side of the mill. I looked around to see if someone was watching us, but we were alone.
"August, try one too. It's fun!" Hugo said.
"I'll aim for the window," I said.
"That's pretty high up."
I threw the egg and missed the window. But I hit the wall with a great splash.
"Can we try another one?" I begged.
"No, Dad will suspect something. Let's go back."

He handed the packages back to me and jumped on the bike. At home he said that he accidentally broke the eggs after he left the store. Dad did not make a fuss, to my surprise. We could do some more throwing next time.

Mom came back from the grocery store with many cans of food, mostly beans. She also bought several pounds of sugar, and complained how hard it was to find sugar in the stores.
She told me that there was a special announcement on the radio to store food items that were easy to keep. We had to put them in boxes so we could easily take them to the shelter.
"Why do we need to do this, Mom?" I asked her.
"There may be war," she says.
She hesitated for a moment, noticing my surprise. I didn't hear anything about it at school.
"There are ships on the ocean that carry bombs and America and Russia may use those bombs. Everybody hopes that they won't because the bombs are very big. They are special, atomic bombs."
She frowned and pursed her lips. She looked at me seriously, putting her hand on my shoulder.
"Am I going to get off from school?" I asked.
Mom broke into a smile. She squeezed my shoulder and said: "There is no reason for you to not go to school tomorrow."
I was disappointed about school but her gentle squeeze reassured me. The bombs no longer frightened me.
Dad came in with empty containers for Agfa photo paper. They were large cans, made out of tin, bright orange on the outside and shiny gold on the inside.
"Here, Riny, these should be good," he said. "I emptied three of them."

Mom started packing the cans and sugar in the boxes. I picked up the small cans and handed them to her.
Then my father said with a grave voice: "I hope the Russians will turn their ships around."
I looked at him, wondering why they wouldn't do that. It sounded simple to me.
At bedtime, Mom told me not to worry. But I noticed that she hugged me longer than normal.
Two days later I saw that Dad was smiling. The ships had turned around.

Church bells were ringing around the city. The Queen Mother, Princess Wilhelmina, had died. Her funeral was on TV. All guests were wearing white because Wilhelmina had requested it. She didn't want the funeral to look like a sad occasion.
Dad was talking about Queen Wilhelmina during the war.
Winston Churchill called her 'the only man in my War cabinet,' he said solemnly.
"She couldn't stand the Germans after they invaded. She took the invasion as a personal insult. After the war, Wilhelmina wanted to remove German from school curriculums and she almost succeeded. She was quite a lady...."
"Why did Churchill call her a 'man'?" I asked.
"Well, it's an expression, August. It means she had a strong personality."
Puzzled, I continued watch the funeral on TV.

7

American Cornflakes

Winter was severe in 1963. We did not have school for several days because of the cold and, for the first time in five years, the *Elfstedentocht* was held. The skaters left around four o'clock in the morning. It was dark, windy and bitterly cold. Only one out of ten skaters completed the race that connects the eleven major towns in the Dutch province of Friesland. I followed the finish of the race on the radio. A skater from Friesland, Reinier Paping, won and Queen Juliana was present to welcome him at the finish line. As the crowd surrounding the Queen became bigger, the ice began to crack. They were barely able to move the Queen off the ice in time. In newspaper pictures the next day, Paping looked exhausted with ice hanging from his eyebrows, as bystanders support him.

Several weeks later I noticed that Reinier Paping was advertising Brinta in Het Handelsblad, our newspaper. Brinta was the cereal that Mom wanted me to eat every morning. She said it was healthy. I didn't like it, because it was gooey and tasted like porridge. To Mom's surprise, I asked for Brinta the next morning.

The Westersingel canal had been frozen solid for six weeks. The canal was not as busy with skaters anymore because people were getting bored. Hugo and I strapped skates around our regular shoes. Hugo helped me to get the leather straps on tightly so my skates didn't slide. We were not the only

ones on the ice with strap-on skates, but most kids had steel skates with built-in shoes. Hugo and I had begged Mom and Dad for steel Norwegian skates but we didn't get them. We made Mom and Dad promise that we could get them next year.
I loved the games of ice hockey with neighborhood kids. We used tree branches as sticks and tried to hit a rubber ball. Our goals were thick pieces of wood, frozen upright in the ice. We loved to play in the evening with street lights shining on the ice just enough to see the ball.

Usually, Mom would come out of the house around seven.
"August, time for dinner!" she'd yell.
I said goodbye to my friends and headed off the ice.
"Was it fun tonight?" Mom asked.
"Yeah, we had a good game. I almost scored two goals, Mom!"
"August, wash your hands before dinner. Right now."
I ran up the stairs to go to the bathroom. When I picked up the soap I noticed Mom's medicine.
"Mom, you left your medicine out here!"
She came upstairs very quickly and, out of breath, grabbed the medicine.
"Thanks, August. Never take any of this."
"OK, Mom."
She held the two boxes firmly in her hand.
"I forgot to take them away," she said apologetically.
She went to her bedroom and I heard the drawer of her nightstand open and close. That's where Mom kept her medicine.
She came back into the bathroom and smiled at me.
"Don't you wish this winter was over, August? It's so cold. We're using twice as much coal as last year."
"I like putting coals into the furnace," I said.
"I look forward to the lilacs blooming in the backyard," she said, staring out the window.
"I like the way the lilacs smell," I said.
"August, do you think we should get more lilac bushes?"
"Yeah. About ten of them, all over the yard."
"Maybe we'll plant some this spring."

We often had fried potatoes, my favorite food. Mom cut the leftover potatoes from the night before into flakes, frying them with lots of butter in our large blue pan. When I smelled the potatoes I rushed into the kitchen to see what she was doing.

"Can I help?" I asked.
"Sure, August. Take the large wooden spoon and make sure it's not cooking too fast. Flip the potatoes when they're brown."
Standing on a chair, I proudly stirred the potatoes.
"You are a good cook, August!" Mom said.
At dinner, the potatoes tasted great. I had stirred them.

It was early spring. The buds on the lilac bushes were the first in our yard. The long winter was over. It had not been this cold in twenty-five years. We could keep the outside doors to the back porch wide open again. Dad was making coffee while we ate lunch. He loved coffee. Cranking a handle, he ground the beans in a green plastic container. He put a filter on top of the dark blue coffee pot and filled it with his finely ground coffee. Then he carefully poured hot water until the small pot was filled to the rim. Because Mom couldn't drink coffee anymore because of her medicine, so Dad drank the pot all by himself.

Mom missed coffee. She begged her doctor several times for a small exception but he had been very strict with her.
I loved to eat coffee beans. I would eat them like candy.
"Coffee is not for children and you should not eat the beans, August," Dad said.
"I love to crack them with my teeth."
"One day you'll lose a tooth," Mom said.
"My teeth are fine," I said as I went back into the kitchen, looking for loose beans.

Chewing on a bean, I went into the backyard. The sun was shining into my eyes and I tried to look beyond the outside wall in our backyard. The wall was made of slabs of gray concrete, which slid into heavy concrete pillars. On the left side, the top slab was detached from the pillar. I used the small opening as a foothold to climb over the wall, counting on the slab to stay in place. Then I would jump down onto the path behind our house. This was the way to visit my friend Eddy who lived two streets down. Dad was not happy that Eddy was my friend. He told me that Eddy's family was lower class and that I should not be hanging around their house. Because Eddy and I had fun together, I never told Dad when I was off to see him.

When I was not playing with Eddy I set up my soccer goal in the backyard. It was made out of broomstick handles,

with leftover white sheers as goal nets. My red ball was just the right size for the goal. I played the Dutch soccer competition with eighteen teams. I kept scores diligently, writing them down in a book, complete with half-time scores and the names of the people who scored. I always made sure that my favorite team, Ajax Amsterdam, would win the overall competition. When I came back into the house, Dad would tell me that he didn't understand why I was so crazy about soccer.
"I find pieces of paper with soccer scores all over the house. It drives me nuts!" he said.
"Dad, I can't help it that you don't like soccer."
"Do you have to write down the scores all the time?" he would ask.
"Yes, it's part of the game."
"At least clean up this stuff in the corner. Your Mom does not want to see these pieces of paper around."
"OK. I'll put them in my soccer book."
Dutifully, I gathered the many small pieces of paper and put them in my book.
"Doesn't that look a lot better?" Dad asked.
"I guess so. Tomorrow I'll start with the English league game. That's an even bigger competition than the Dutch league," I told him.
"Yeah, sure," my father said as he headed for the kitchen. Then he turned around and said: "August, isn't there anything better you could do with your time?"
"No, Dad. I like this."
Without saying a word, Dad went into the kitchen.
I wondered if there would be enough time to start the English league before dinner.

May 4 was Memorial Day, the solemn commemoration of people who died in World War II. At seven in the evening, the TV broadcast of the official ceremony started. My parents watched in a grave mood as war survivors slowly marched up the Waalsdorper dunes on the Atlantic coast near The Hague. The veterans carried candles and the procession finally made its way to the top. Wreaths were laid at the memorial site and a soldier played the Last Post. There was a minute of silence. I was afraid to make a sound because Mom and Dad were staring intently at the screen.
I had never been to the beach on the Atlantic Coast. We never went on vacation.

The broadcast of the survivors' ceremony was always followed by special war documentaries. We would see the familiar pictures of the bombing of Rotterdam, Holland's capitulation to the German Army, the famous battles in Europe, finally followed by detailed accounts of the German concentration camps.
"The kids shouldn't be watching this, Charles!" Mom would exclaim.
"You're right, Riny."
But my parents never changed the program or sent me off to bed. The people in pajamas with thin bodies and frightened faces looked strange but they did not scare me.

At the end of the documentary, they showed the cleanup of the camps. When nude bodies were swung onto carts it became too much for me and I left the room quietly to go to bed. That night, I would dream about the bodies on the carts.

In June, during the last days of second grade when I was seven years old, Mom came back from the Albert Heijn grocery store with a new cereal.
"It's from America. They call it Cornflakes. It's supposed to be healthy."
I looked at the enormous box with many little, yellow flakes.
"Can I try some, Mom?"
"Yes, August, of course. You can put some sugar on it, too. I have heard that people do that."
I took a big spoon and started eating the new food. With lots of sugar. It was just like candy, much better than the Brinta porridge.
"Can we have this instead of Brinta, Mom? Please, please." I begged.
"We'll see, August. This American food is not as healthy as Brinta. Certainly not with these loads of sugar."
"Please, Mom. I won't put on as much next time."
She was not convinced.

We finished the box of Cornflakes in two days. Then Brinta came back again. It would take several years before Cornflakes became our regular breakfast.

8

A Special Mass

I was slowly waking up. It was a Saturday at the end of November. I was eight years old. The gifts from Sinterklaas were still two weeks away. It was cold. I didn't want to get up to go to Saturday morning school. Hugo was stirring in his bed. He was awake.
"August, wake up! I want to tell you something," he said.
"Huh? What is it?"
"The President of the United States, Kennedy, was killed yesterday. They announced it on the late news last night," Hugo said.
He had an air of importance.
"They caught the man who killed him, Lee Harvey Oswald," he continued.
His pronunciation of English names was excellent.
Without an answer, I turned around and went back to sleep.

On Sunday morning, Mom told me that we would go to High Mass at ten.
"Because of the American President," she said quietly.
Dad stayed home, as usual, smoking tobacco.
We went early, and managed to get seats in the back. It was very busy. We were not the only ones who had decided to go to High Mass. Many people were lighting candles and though the church was packed it was very quiet.

"*....Domine Deus, Agnus Dei, Filius Patris, qui tollis peccata mundi, miserere nobis; qui tollis peccata mundi, suscipe deprecationem nostram. Qui sedes ad dexteram Patris, misere nobis.*"

We prayed louder than normal, and I joined in with my favorite '*qui tollis peccata mundi.*' In Latin, the rest of the *Gloria* went too fast for me.

Mom had planned to light a candle for President Kennedy at the end of the Mass but the line was long and she didn't want to wait.

"We'll do it next time," she said.

Later that day, we watched the evening news. The announcer said that Lee Harvey Oswald had been shot and taken to the same hospital where President Kennedy had died two days earlier. Before he could finish the prepared text, someone handed him a piece of paper. He glanced at it for a second and then said in a somber tone: "We just received word that Lee Harvey Oswald has died from his gunshot wound."

"Now they will never know what happened!" my father exclaimed.

Everybody was quiet and we watched the rest of the TV program without real interest. Then Mom got up.

"August, time for bed," she said.

"Oh Mom, can I stay up a little longer? They may have more on President Kennedy."

"No, it's your bedtime now," she said firmly.

Mom promised to kiss me goodnight and I went upstairs to brush my teeth.

In bed, I hugged my teddy bear and called for Mom. I heard footsteps on the stairs, but it was Dad. I could tell from his slow, heavy walk. When Dad wanted to kiss me goodnight I said, "Your beard is too prickly, I want Mom." He smiled and tried to kiss me anyway as I turned away.

After Dad left the room, I started yelling for Mom. I loved hearing the sound of her quick footsteps on the stairway. She kissed me gently and hugged me, then headed back downstairs. I kept saying "Goodbye Mom, goodbye." She stopped several times on the stairway to say goodbye. Then I heard the living room door open and close.

I turned in my bed and started humming a song. It was loud enough that Mom told me to be quiet from downstairs.

"Come on, August, go to sleep!"

"Goodbye, Mom, goodbye."
"Goodbye, August."
I was humming softly to myself. I could do that for what seemed like hours before I fell asleep.

9

Vacation In Lugano

Dad drew beautiful pencil portraits. Filled with intricate details, they oddly resembled the black and white photographs he worked with everyday. He had learned pencil sketching in his first year at the Art Academy, but left the school after the Depression forced him to help his father in the family photography business.

Twelve years later, after World War II ended, Dad started to paint again. His first painting measured eight feet by twelve feet. He worked on it for months in the attic, the only place in the house that was big enough. It depicted angels, horses in the sky, and lots of people weeping on the side. It was done in the style of the romantic German painter Anselm Feuerbach, Dad's idol. He made the painting to impress a pretty girl he had seen in the photography store. She never saw it. Dad found out she was engaged to a motorcycle driver.

When I was eight years old, Dad began to paint family pictures. He spent a lot of time on the portrait of my mother. It was a view from her right side, with Mom sitting on a chair. A white silk scarf was draped around her head. She looked like Indira Gandhi. When the painting was finished, Mom complained about her large bottom. After much discussion, Dad agreed to take some off. But not much. He claimed that taking off more would not be realistic. He used a photograph of my mom as proof. It didn't convince Mom. She remained unhappy, but Dad refused to change the picture any further.

I hated posing. I always started to cry after a while and it was hard for Dad to photograph my pose. He ended up painting three portraits of me. I loved his last portrait. Staring intently to the left, my mouth looked tense, probably from posing too long. The colors of the painting are very good. I wore a black bow-tie on a white shirt, and a gray sweater. He made my ears exactly the right size. It was me.

Mom complained that our basement was not cold enough for storage and that she needed to go the store almost every day to buy meat. Dad finally relented late in the summer and agreed to buy a refrigerator.
Mom immediately tried out the tiny freezer compartment on the top shelf of the refrigerator. She could squeeze in three packages of meat. That meant she could wait at least three days before she needed to buy meat again. Mom was very happy about it. Dad had to move the refrigerator three times before she was satisfied with its spot in the kitchen.
Mom told us that if we had spare freezer space we could make ice cubes for lemonade.

A few months later, the new breakfront for the living room arrived. Mom had noticed the breakfront in the showroom of a local furniture store and wanted it desperately. Dad told her that it was an expensive piece, but she insisted.
"We need it! We have nothing to keep our good china in!" she said over and over again.
The breakfront was our largest piece of furniture. Behind glass sliding doors it had three racks for our china and a separate pull-out served as a writing desk. Three large storage drawers formed the bottom part of the breakfront.
Mom was surprisingly subdued after the piece was installed in the room. She didn't seem to be happy about it. The next day, I heard her crying.
"I don't want that thing in here," she said through her tears.
"But *Rineke*, you wanted it so badly," Dad said softly.
"I never wanted it. Get it out of here!"
"Let's wait a few days. Maybe you'll like it better then," my father tried.
She got up to go to their bedroom. Dad followed her upstairs. Hugo and I heard his pleading voice through my mother's crying and screaming. She cried for a long time, and Hugo and I decided to go outside.

I was confused. Mom sounded so different from yesterday. It made me sad, as Hugo and I played soccer in the backyard. Dad said there was no way to get rid of the breakfront because we couldn't get a refund or trade-in for some other piece of furniture. We kept it, and Mom hated it.

When I opened the white double doors from the outside, I noticed that Hugo was sitting at the living room table. He was doing homework.
"Hi, August," he said, looking up at me.
"What's up?" I asked.
"I want to tell you something I heard last night. Come with me."
He got up and walked through the open doors to the garage. I dropped my schoolbag and followed him.
"Why are we in the garage, Hugo?"
"I don't want Mom or Dad to hear this," he said secretively.
"Well?" I asked.
"Last night, when I was in the living room finishing my homework, Mom and Dad were talking in the kitchen about their visit to the specialist."
I had heard the word 'specialist' before but I wasn't sure what it meant.
"Who is the specialist?"
"Dr. Klein works especially with people who have problems like Mom's and he knows more about it than Dr. Boom. Mom is still not feeling well, so she went to Dr. Klein," Hugo explained.
"What did the new doctor say?"
"Well, last night Mom said that she wasn't happy with the new doctor. He wants her to change her medication. Mom thinks it is not going to make any difference. Dad tried to tell her that the doctor knows best and that Dr. Klein thinks that Mom has too much stress. She needs to do less household chores and should not help out in Dad's business. As long as she gets enough sleep with the new medication, she should be fine. She got very upset when Dad said that she just needed more sleep. 'It's not just sleep! It's much more!' she said and she started to cry. Then she ran out of the kitchen and went to bed. Dad came into the living room a few minutes later and was surprised to see me. 'Hugo, it's late. Please go upstairs,' he said. I cleaned up my things and went upstairs. Mom was crying in the bedroom."
"What do you think of it, Hugo?" I asked.

"I don't know. I don't like it," Hugo said quietly.
"Does it have to do with us?"
He looked at me for a second and got up, walking back to the house.
"I don't think so. Don't worry about it."
    I had been sitting near the coals in the garage and my hands were black from the dust. I quickly went to the kitchen to wash my hands. Mom would be furious if she saw my dirty hands.

    On Sundays during summer, Mom, Hugo, and I biked to the local swimming pool, the Welborn. Mom made omelet sandwiches and, on our way to the pool, we visited the new Catholic church at the outskirts of town. It was less official than St. Barbara's and they played the guitar instead of the church organ.
    At the swimming pool, Mom spread out the big purple towel on the pool lawn and started sun bathing. I went into the water and raced back to her many times to tell her what had happened in the water. She smiled.
"Please, Mom. Can you go with me?" I begged.
"No, August. I'm comfortable here. Just go ahead."
"But Mom, it's so much fun on the slide. Please."
"Just go ahead. I'll be right here."
I raced to find Hugo who was at the deep end of the pool. We had a great time running around and diving into the water.
    At the end of the afternoon, Mom picked up our stuff. We had eaten all of the omelet sandwiches and the lemonade was gone. I noticed that Mom paused before she got on her bike, as if she was catching her breath. After she got going, I jumped on the back of her bike for the ride home. Hugo followed on his dark blue bike. Mom's long summer dress covered my legs as the wind blew.

    Late in the summer of 1964, we watched the Tokyo Olympics on TV. Because of the time difference with Japan, I was in front of the TV early in the morning, before I had to leave for school.
    On the first day, the Dutch bicycling time trial team won a gold medal. Surprisingly, the Dutch field hockey team had trouble beating the Japanese team. The Japanese, although new at field hockey, threw themselves fanatically into the Dutch shots. Their exuberance startled and rattled the Dutch team.

Bob Hayes from the U.S. was my idol in the 100 meters dash. He ran 10.0 seconds for the gold medal, equaling the world record.

Anton Geesink won a second gold medal for Holland in judo. He got his Japanese opponent into a holding grip, maintaining it for the required few seconds. The Dutch fans stormed onto the mat to embrace Geesink, but he waved them back into the stands. Calmly, he knelt down to rearrange his shirt. Then he got up and bowed to his opponent. He waved to the supporters to come forward now and they lifted him on their shoulders in triumph. Geesink was hailed in Japan because of the respect he showed for his opponent at the end of his victorious match.

Mom hardly watched the Olympics. She had trouble sleeping and the doctor couldn't find the right medication. She looked gaunt and tired when she got up in the morning. Some mornings, I could hear Dad talk to her in his hushed voice in their bedroom. It sounded like he was asking her something. Usually there was no answer. When my father came out of the bedroom, he was smoking a cigarette and his head was down. He looked up when he saw me.

"How are you, August?"

"I'm fine, Dad."

I was trying to stay out of his smoke.

"What do you have in school this morning?" he asked.

"Eh, eh… I don't know. I can look it up."

"That's OK, August," he says in an understanding voice.

He never asked this before. He only talked about school when I received my report card.

He wanted to make things appear normal but I knew they weren't.

"I hate that Van Eerden. He keeps me from doing my work with his endless chit-chat about his family. Just as I get going he'll walk by and ruin my day. Damn it!"

Opa Brouwers was furious, and he was pacing back and forth in the room.

"Nobody cares. I'm sick of it!" he thundered.

I was scared and Aunt Netty was holding me tight. I could feel she was also scared of Opa.

"That stupid work in the factory, it amounts to nothing. Do you understand?!"

"Oh, calm down, man!" Oma said angrily.

But Opa just kept on going, pacing back and forth.
"I'm sick of it. I'm sick of it. Damn it!" he shouted even louder than before.
My aunt squeezed me harder and I felt trapped. I had trouble breathing. I had never seen Opa like this.
"I could give a damn!" he said as he opened the door to the hallway.
"And I don't give a f--- about all of you!"
He closed the door hard behind him. It was over.
"He'll just stay in bed for the next two days," Oma sighed. She was calm, she had seen it before.
"When the leaves start to fall he goes crazy. It's always the same," she said.

Aunt Netty got up and finally let go of me. I raced outside to play with the pebbles in the backyard. I felt I had just seen a person I didn't know but who looked like Opa Brouwers.

Oma told me that I looked just like Mom.
"You have your mother's eyes. And your skin is dark, just like hers."
She found a picture when Mom was my age.
"See how much you look like her."
I didn't see the resemblance.
"August, because of your dark skin it's easy for you to get a tan, just like your mom."
"Oma, my skin isn't dark. It's yellow."
Oma laughed.
"OK, but it looks fine to me," she said.

On Monday nights, I had soccer practice. I played for Fortitudo, the Catholic soccer club in Culemborg. It took twenty-five minutes by bike to get to the practice field at the other end of town. Two blocks down from us were the soccer fields of Vriendenschaar, the Protestant team. I begged Dad to let me play there because it would be easy to get to practice.
"I will not have you play for a Protestant team. And that's that!" he said sternly. The teachers at Dad's Catholic school successfully shaped in his mind a devilish image of Martin Luther. Dad viewed Catholicism as the "true" religion and he had no good words for any of the Protestant varieties. He talked seriously about the Index, the official list of books banned by the Catholic Church. When the Pope was on TV, blessing the crowds at St. Peter's Square, he got up from his chair, making

the sign of the cross as if he were standing right in front of the pontiff. At home, he was a strong believer. But he never went to church. There was no way I would ever be allowed to join Protestant Vriendenschaar.

Fortitudo's practice field was called "The Hill" because the field had many hills -- and holes -- and only half of it had grass. The other half was mud, except in the middle of summer, when the dirt was as hard as concrete. There were never nets in the goals for practice: they were put in only for the matches on Saturdays and Sundays.

Our coach was Wout Dorresteijn, the son of the pharmacist whose store was at the corner, one block down from our house. Sometimes, Wout was in the store. He was a head taller than his father and he had a strong, deep voice. At practice, he started by making us run around the field twice. After that, I was too tired to do well on the first ball exercise. Wout was strict about teaching soccer fundamentals. He spent a large part of practice on learning how to trap the ball. I got nervous when he came around to check how we were doing. When I missed one ball, he immediately shouted at me.
"Pay attention! Keep your foot down!"
After his comment I improved, particularly when he was watching.
I played midfield. All boys on my team wore a number on the back of their shirt. I was the only one who didn't have one. Every week after practice I asked Mom.
"Mom, can you put on number seven, please?"
"No, August, not now, I'm busy," she said.
"But everyone else has one," I continued.
"Maybe later," she said after a while.
Carefully, I put my number back in the side pocket of my bag.
One night, a Volkswagen van parked in front of our house. Wout came out of the car and rang the front door. Mom opened the door.
"Mrs. Swanenberg, can August play tonight? I know this is not his regular team but we are one person short and we are playing at Everdingen. He'll be back at eight-thirty."
"It's OK with me. August, do you want to play?" Mom asked.
"Yes, yes!"
I ran up the stairs to get my white shorts and light blue shirt.
In the match with Everdingen I scored two goals and I had one assist. We won 4-3. At home, after the match, I told Mom about my game.

"Mom, can you sew the number on now?"
"Maybe tomorrow, August," Mom said.
She hated sewing.

In the early fall of 1964, when I turned nine years old, I played in the City Championships for school teams. My school, St. Willibrord, was one of the favorites to win the tournament. We had a slow start in the first match against St. Augustine, Culemborg's other Catholic school. Lucky to be at 0-0, we got a cornerkick just before halftime. The ball somehow landed on my forehead and from there into the goal. I did not move my head: I was too amazed by what had happened. I had scored the first goal. On the sideline, Hugo shouted his congratulations. I was too dizzy from the ball hitting my head to answer him. I needed most of the second half to recover from my surprise header. We ended up winning the match, 2-0.

We reached the City finals, which were played on Vriendenschaar's main field. The grandstand was filled with 250 people as we battled the Scheffel public school. They were a tough team because they had several Moluccan players who were quick and skillful with the ball. I was so nervous that I hardly touched the ball, let alone scored a goal. Our star player, Jonnie, was in great form and scored both goals in our 2-1 win. We received the City Cup from the mayor of Culemborg. Jonnie deserved to hold the Cup. And he did, the whole time.

My parents didn't go to the final game and Hugo was away, visiting with friends. The other kids on my team were too busy talking to their parents and other family members. I quickly left for home.

I overheard Mom and Dad talking about a trip to Switzerland. They were in their bedroom when I came up the stairs after school.
"Riny, Lugano is beautiful. It's on the lake."
"When are we leaving?" Mom asked.
"In the fall, after the busy season. Louis will drive."
"What about the kids?"
"They can stay with your family. It's only two weeks."
Silence.
"Riny, aren't you excited?"
I heard Mom get up from the bed. Quickly, I went into my bedroom.

I asked Hugo about it and he already knew that he and I were not going. He said that Uncle Louis was taking Mom and Dad to his vacation home in Lugano, Switzerland. We were to stay with Oma and Opa Brouwers in Tiel, out old hometown.
I felt very disappointed. I had never been outside Holland. I couldn't believe they were not taking us, but I was afraid to talk about it with them. For several days, I wondered if Mom and Dad would tell me, clinging to the hope that I would be going too.
One day, when I came home, Mom was sitting at the dining room table. She had just prepared lunch.
I walked right up to her.
"Are we going with you to Switzerland?" I asked.
Mom looked up and said quietly "No, August. Not this time."
"That's not fair," I said.
I was mad and I looked straight at her.
Mom started to cry. She held her hands in her face. She couldn't talk anymore.
I groaned and ran out of the house, determined to stay away from lunch.
Later that day, Hugo told me that the trip was a special present for Mom because she wasn't feeling well. I was not to make any more comments about it to her, he said.

When my parents returned from Switzerland, Mom had a beautiful tan. She didn't look tired anymore.
A week later we had a slide show in our living room. Dad set up the projector. Sliding the pictures into the holder one by one he showed us all their pictures. I liked the pictures of Nancy, France. My parents had passed through the city on Armistice Day and the downtown buildings had been decorated with blue-white-red French flags. It was the Dutch flag turned upside down. There were lots of pictures of Mom and Dad hiking in the gorgeous Swiss mountains. Lago Maggiore, the great lake at the border between Switzerland and Italy, was beautiful at sunset. The water appeared orange in color, casting a wonderful glow.
I was still mad that my parents had not let me go on the trip, but Hugo told me to shut up because of Mom. I complained a lot to Oma.
She said that I would be going next time, but I didn't believe her.

Today, Mom came back from another doctor's visit. She never said anything about her visits but Hugo told me that Mom would be taking more sleeping pills. Because Mom was awake most of the night, Dad wasn't getting much sleep either. When he came down for breakfast, he went into the kitchen to make tea. Hugo and I could hear him mumbling to himself: "When is this going to stop?"
We looked at each other, not knowing what to say.
We ate our breakfast in silence.
Mom was still in bed when we went to school.

10

The Trip To Vught

In the beginning of 1965, Mom slashed her wrists twice, using razor blades. The first time she only cut herself a bit and Dad made sure to put his razor blades out of reach. Three weeks later, Mom found a used blade and cut herself again. Dad stopped the bleeding by wrapping strips of sheets tightly around her wrist. He held her arm in the bathtub because it was bleeding so much.

When I came home from school a few days later, Mom was gone. Dad told me that she was at a special hospital in Vught. It would be awhile before she'd be back. Dad explained that it had been too difficult for Mom to say goodbye to Hugo and me.
"How long is she going to be there?" I demanded.
"August, it's hard to tell. At least two months. She may be coming home for weekends soon."
"Can we visit her?"
"Yes, I am talking to Uncle Louis to see when we can go. He'll be driving us to Vught. Maybe in three weeks."
"Three weeks. That's a long time. Why?"
"I know, August. We are all trying to do our best."
Dad turned away, his head down, and went upstairs to the dark room.
"Can I stay at Oma's, Dad?"
He didn't turn around.

"Maybe soon, August," he said quietly. I didn't like the sound of his voice.
I wondered what Hugo would have to say about all this.

A serious-looking man dressed in a green uniform opened the heavy gate. Our car moved slowly onto the main road of the institution's courtyard at Vught. Stately rows of oak trees lined numerous foot paths. A half dozen single-story brick buildings were scattered across the grounds. Uncle Louis and Dad sat in the front seats of my uncle's Peugeot. Hugo and I had the back seat to ourselves. We were visiting Mom for the first time. To our surprise she was outside, walking alone on one of the paths.
"Oh, God, it's Riny!" my father exclaimed.
My uncle drove the car close to where Mom was, and stopped. She put one hand on the car and quickly glanced at us. Then she pointed to the bottom part of her nylon stockings. "See, it's all torn! Isn't horrible," she said.
"Hi, Mom," I said. She didn't answer. She continued complaining about the stockings. I didn't think she recognized me. I felt strange and looked at Hugo who shrugged his shoulders. Mom turned away, and said quietly: "I am going to my room now."

We followed slowly behind her in the car until we reached her building. We parked the car and went inside to see her room. It was small and had steel bars on the window.
After a while, Dad, Hugo and Uncle Louis left Mom's room to speak to a nurse. Inside, I was alone with Mom. I asked her about the books in her room, but her answers were absent-minded. Why? She looked so normal.
After a while she mumbled something to herself but I couldn't hear what she said.
Soon, the others came back, telling me that it was time to go home. Mom gave me a quick kiss and said good-bye.
On the way out, Dad told us that it would probably be a little while before she was going to be back home. In a hushed voice, I heard him say to my uncle: "Why did she have to start complaining about her nylons?"
During the drive home I kept thinking about the bars in the window.

Over the next weeks, Dad cooked dinner every night. Sometimes Hugo pitched in, making dinner between homework assignments. I played a lot with my Dinky Toys and built armies with my green plastic soldiers. Dad gave me extra money to buy more soldiers. During the weekends Hugo studied hard, making up for the time lost doing errands. Dad didn't seem to be very busy developing photos. He was staying out of sight, working upstairs on the model train, his main hobby in the slow months. I was usually the only one in the living room. Often, I thought about Mom in that other place. I wished we could visit more, but Dad said that we couldn't go every week. Spending hours with my toy soldiers, the military battles were becoming ever larger and more involved.

Little was said during meals. Hugo would be off to his desk as soon as we were done. He spent a lot of time on math. Dad sounded worried when he asked Hugo about school.
"How is it going?"
"OK, I guess," Hugo answered nonchalantly.
"Are you keeping up?"
"As long as I study hard on the weekends."
"Good. Don't let us down, Hugo."
Dad had a threatening tone in his voice when he said that. He had always been serious about school but now it was even stronger. He never asked me about school. He didn't seem to worry about grade school.

Five weeks after she left us, Mom returned home from the special hospital in Vught. She looked tired and drawn. She didn't say much and mechanically went through her chores at home. One morning, Dad couldn't wake her up. He called an ambulance. Mom had taken an overdose of sleeping pills. At the hospital they pumped her stomach and she was safe. To make sure she was not going to harm herself again the doctors decided to keep her in a special section of the hospital for a while. Dad said that Mom was in there because she was not feeling well, but he didn't talk much about it. Hugo told me that Mom was 'overstressed' but I didn't understand what he meant. And I was afraid to ask.

Dad, Hugo and I visited Mom in the hospital, usually in the evening. The hospital was less than ten minutes from our home by bike. Mom looked better now, calm and rested. She was sleeping well in the hospital but I knew she was getting a lot of pills. Her eyelids were down a bit, even during the day.

One Sunday afternoon, the Dutch soccer team played a big match against Switzerland to qualify for the World Cup. At half time, the score was 0-0. Holland would reach the final round of the World Cup if we could beat the Swiss. I had looked forward to this game for weeks and loved watching the tense first half.
Dad and Hugo were not visiting Mom. Dad was upstairs, out of sight, and Hugo was cramming for an exam on Monday. I felt bad for Mom. She would have no visitors. I got up and turned off the TV, walked to the kitchen and picked up my boots. I shouted to Hugo that I was going to the hospital and he grunted back "That's fine."

It was very cold and the snow was frozen. My bike had a flat tire and I walked the two miles to the hospital, slipping on the icy sidewalks several times. The nurse at the hospital reception nodded her head. She had seen me before. I went upstairs to the end of the hallway. I knew the way. I felt shy walking in because my mother shared her room with three other women. Sitting upright in her bed against two pillows, she smiled when she saw me. I leaned against her bed, while the other women in the room were saying "Oh, how sweet!"
"How are you doing?" she asked me.
I didn't know what to say. I wanted to ask her the same thing.
After a pause, I told her that I was watching the soccer game and that I left at halftime to see her.
"Oh August, you shouldn't have done that. That wasn't necessary!" She knew how much I loved soccer.
I motioned to the flowers we had given her the day before. Yellow chrysanthemums in a black vase. Mom said she really liked them.
"How is Hugo doing?" she asked.
"Oh, he's fine. He is doing his homework this afternoon."
I touched the sheets on her bed. They looked so white and clean. On the nightstand was a pot of chamomile tea; I tasted some from Mom's cup. It had a strong medicinal flavor and I made an ugly face when I swallowed the tea. Mom smiled.
"Are you going to be a good boy, August?" she asked.
"Yes, Mom."
I told her that I had to go and gave her a quick kiss.
"Bye, August. Thanks for visiting me."
"Bye, Mom."
The soccer match was over by the time I got home. Holland lost.

The next week, Mom went straight from the hospital in Culemborg to the institution in Vught. Dad said that we would not be able to visit her for a few weeks. He believed that our visits didn't help Mom. Three weeks later, in early December, she came home for the weekend. She was not feeling well and stayed in bed most of the time. On Sunday afternoon she returned to Vught, saying goodbye before getting into the car of Uncle Louis's car.
"August, be a good boy now."
"Yes, Mom."
She gave Hugo and me a hurried kiss on the cheek and waved to Dad. The she turned abruptly to the car.
She didn't look back.
The car moved slowly around the curve to the Keestra Singel. I ran to the corner, watching the car until it was out of view, beyond the canal.
I forgot to wave.

In the last weeks of December, Mom was feeling better. She'd be coming home for the holidays from Christmas through New Year's Day. She would return to Vught the day after New Year's Day.
I was out the salon, looking out the window, waiting for my Uncle Louis' Peugeot to arrive with Mom. She was early and I ran to the front door.
"Hi Mom!"
"Hello, August."
She looked good and she was smiling. It made me happy.
She grabbed me at the waist and gave me a big kiss.
"I am happy to see you again," she said and she hugged me.
Hugo and Dad had come to the front door and were behind me. Everybody was together again.
Dad went into the kitchen to make coffee, while Hugo and I took Mom with us into the living room.
"How are things at school?" she asked.
I showed her my Christmas report card. I was proud of it.
"This time, I even have a nine for religion, Mom."
"You are a good boy, August."
Hugo showed his report card next. It was good and she congratulated him.
"I have to go upstairs and put my things away," she suddenly said in a hurried voice. She put out her cigarette, picked up her bag and went upstairs to the bedroom.

After she left, Dad came into the room with the coffee.
"Where is Riny?" he asked.
"She went upstairs to unpack her bags," Hugo said.
Dad hesitated.
"I'll have the coffee later," he said in a serious voice. Quickly, he went upstairs.

After five minutes, Dad returned alone. He said that Mom was in the bedroom, sound asleep. The trip from Vught had worn her out. She came downstairs for dinner, looking rested and seemed to be in a good mood. Dad was relieved. After dinner we had lemonade with cookies. I told Mom about my soccer team, and how we won our last game.
She asked more questions than she had in a long time.

The next day, Hugo and I went to Christmas Mass. It was a busy Mass. Back home I told Mom about it.
"Father Stricker did the sermon, Mom."
"He's your favorite, isn't he, August?"
"Yes, he's nice. I always go to him for Confession."
"What did he talk about in the sermon?"
"Oh, I forgot. It was a really long one, Mom. Maybe Hugo knows."
"That's fine, August."
"They had a neat manger display, Mom. The ox and donkey were really big. And the Magi were on camels."
"Sounds like I missed something today."
"You did, Mom, you did!" I exclaimed.
Suddenly, she looked sad.
"Mom, I am going to play with my Dinky Toys now."
"OK, August."

For most of the week Mom was in good spirits. She helped out in the kitchen and set the dinner table. I overheard Dad say to Hugo that Mom was much better this time. On New Year's Eve, we went out at midnight to watch the fireworks light the sky across our town. Dad looked at the fireworks for a short time and then decided to go to bed. He never liked holidays.

Mom was not used to the late hour. She felt sleepy but she stayed up to see Hugo's fireworks launched from a bottle in the backyard. We watched the golden stars shoot high into the sky. After the fireworks we went back inside to eat the *oliebollen* doughnuts that Mom had made for us.

The Trip To Vught 67

New Year's Day dawned dreary and cloudy with a little rain. Dinner was early because Mom would be going back to Vught the next morning. She smiled a lot during the meal and laughed when we told her about the Thunderstrike firecrackers we had set off in downtown Culemborg earlier that day. I felt sad that she had to leave. I liked her visit very much.
After dinner, Mom went upstairs to pack. I followed to help her get ready. Upstairs, she told me that she did not want to go back to Vught.
   I got bored after helping Mom pack some of her clothes, and started looking for fun things in her closet. Mom's wooden jewelry box was just within my reach. She told me she had not used it in a long time. I loved the pearl on the silver pin and I held it against the light to see the colored reflections on the pearl. I smelled the pin's black, tarnished silver.
"Can I have it when I grow up?" I asked.
"Are you going to be careful with it, August?"
"Oh yes. For sure."
"Then you can have it now."
Holding the pin, I ran down the stairs to tell Hugo and Dad.
"Mom will let me have this pin!"
"Really?" Dad asked, surprised.
"Yes. She told me I can have it."

   That night Mom came upstairs to my room to say goodnight. She was done packing for her trip.
"Thanks for helping me, August," she said.
"Mom, can I really have your pin?"
"Of course, August. I promised it, didn't I?"
"Yes. Thank you."
I looked toward the ceiling and pictured the silver pin with the pearl. "Goodnight, August."
Mom leaned over and gave me a hug and two kisses.
"I'll see you in the morning, August."
"Goodnight, Mom."
She closed the door carefully.
"Goodnight, Mom, goodnight."
She stopped on the stairway to say one more 'goodnight.'
Then I heard more footsteps.
And the door of the living room opened and closed.

11

January 2, 1966

I woke up late and heard voices on the street. I crawled on my bed to the window to find out who was outside. A man holding a green bottle was opening the driver's side door of a car I did not recognize. Dad was helping Mom get into the car. After Dad got into the backseat with Mom the car drove off very quickly.

Then I heard Hugo coming up the stairs. "Quick, get dressed! We need to go to the hospital!" he said. I was afraid to ask why. Just two months before, Mom had been in the hospital for an overdose of sleeping pills. With me on the back, Hugo rode his bike as fast as he could to the hospital. I felt nervous about going to the hospital, barely managing to hold onto the seat as we bounced with every bump in the road.

At the hospital we ran to the emergency room. A nurse opened the doors to a large room where Dad stood at Mom's bedside. He was wearing his green raincoat, and his hands were folded in prayer. Next to him, a priest was saying the Last Rites. Mom was wildly moving her head back and forth, gasping for air. Her eyes were wide open, in a fixed, unrecognizing gaze. The nurse, holding Mom's hands, was struggling to restrain her.

I did not want to get closer. Mumbling his prayers quietly, the priest looked far removed from Mom's pain. I was mad at the priest for not doing much. He was just holding his book.

I turned around and left the room. I sat down, putting my head on a table and began to cry, ever louder. A nurse came and softly put her hand on my shoulder. After a while I stopped crying and stared ahead of me. The head nurse took me to the priest who had said the Last Rites. He had just returned to his hospital office. Another nurse came in with the priest's meal. The priest was fat and short and talked without looking at me, carefully eating his meatball with brown sauce. I couldn't get Mom's heavy breathing out of my mind. And her stare. I was sure she had not recognized me.

Uncle Louis picked me up from the priest's office. We were going to drive with Dad to the Academic Hospital in Utrecht, where Mom had been taken by ambulance. Heavy rain was coming down. We were silent. My uncle was driving fast, passing cars on the wet highway. I could see the speedometer from my back seat: 140, sometimes 150 kilometers per hour, as I watched the raindrops being blown around on the windows.

We arrived in Utrecht and Uncle Louis parked in front of the hospital. Dad told me to stay in the car. He and Uncle Louis went into the hospital.

I waited for two hours. The rain continued to pour.

When they finally returned, Dad's head was down.

He said: "Mom is seriously ill."

"How bad is it?" I asked.

"It's serious. Very serious," Dad said in a grave tone.

No one spoke in the car on the drive back to Culemborg. When we arrived home the rain had stopped but the clouds made it dark already. Uncle Louis left almost at once. My father sat down at the living room table across from my mother's picture. He looked up and started to cry, exclaiming "Riny, Oh Riny!" I sat opposite from him at the table. His bald head rested on his folded arms. His entire body shook with every cry.

I did not dare move or say anything. The doorbell rang and my father got up to answer it. I heard him speak in hushed tones. I did not know to whom. Something about insurance.

Then he came back and looked sadder than before. He folded his head in his arms again and cried. I looked at some of my favorite things in our living room. The clock with the wooden angel on top, the cups in the glass breakfront and the gray Philips gramophone in the corner. Dad stopped crying and looked at me for a long time, without saying a word. It made me feel uncomfortable.

The doorbell rang again. It was Mr. Mandos, our neighbor, offering his help. He had not been at our house in a long time.

In the evening, Uncle Louis returned and picked me up for a trip to his home in Tiel. I quickly got my clothes ready for a three-day stay. I asked my uncle where Hugo was. He looked at me for a moment and said:
"Your brother was very brave today. He went in the ambulance with your Mom to Utrecht. He is coming back to your home tonight by train from Utrecht."
I had not seen Hugo since we entered the hospital's emergency room in the morning. I missed him.
At my uncle's home, I found a small travel chess set. I didn't know the rules but I loved moving the tiny pieces on the board. Aunt Riet kept asking me if I needed something to eat or drink. She had all kinds of food, candy and drinks, much more than we had at home.
I took the little chess set with me to bed. After my aunt closed the door, I jumped out of bed and turned on the light so I could play with the set. The next morning, I woke up with little chess pieces scattered on my pillow.

Around ten o'clock in the morning Opa arrived.
"Hello, rascal. I'm here to pick you up. You are going to stay with us for a while."
I wanted to ask him about Mom but somehow I couldn't. I was afraid.
"Opa, how long am I staying?"
"Maybe two or three days."

Oma had just made lunch when we arrived. She was toasting bread in the silver toaster. She had bought raisin rolls, my favorites.
After lunch, I asked Oma and Opa where Mom was.
"Oh, my God. You don't know?!" Oma exclaimed.
Opa moved closer to me.
"Your mother is dead," he said.
I put my head in my arms and started crying softly. I was not sad. I was alone.
"The funeral is Wednesday," Oma said. "Do you want to go?"

"No, I don't want to be there! People will be staring at me."
"That's okay," Opa said, "That's okay."
And he put his hand on my shoulder.

12

Sherries And Camel Cigarettes

Mom's funeral was in Tiel. Dad had reserved their spots at the local cemetery years earlier. He had designed the gravestone himself: an elegantly long, white marble cross with triangular gray stones on the sides. The stones left just enough space for the names of the deceased. He had used the same design earlier for the grave of his parents in the same cemetery.

One day after my mom died, Dad and the priest in Tiel discussed the funeral ceremony. "Mr. Swanenberg, you have to understand that the Catholic Church has a history of not allowing full ceremony burial in the case of suicide. Suicide victims used to be buried in plots outside the cemetery grounds," the priest intoned.
He carefully rearranged his black robe.
"Is it possible to have a regular funeral?" Dad asked anxiously.
"I need to look into that. What is the official cause of death?"
Dad handed the priest the death certificate. The priest studied it at length, taking off his large, black glasses. He rubbed his chin slowly and precisely.
"I will talk to our pastor about this. Please call me tomorrow," the priest said officiously.
"Is there anything I can do to help?"
"Yes, maybe," the priest mumbled, putting his glasses back on.
"Mr. Swanenberg, the Church is always grateful for the support offered by its members," the priest said quietly but clearly.

He got up and left the room.
The next morning, Dad called the priest and pledged several special donations. The priest was grateful for the call.
In the afternoon, the Church decided to give Mom a full Catholic funeral service and burial in the Catholic cemetery.

    I stayed with my grandparents in the days before the funeral. On the day before the funeral, Oma returned from church.
"August, your Mom looks so beautiful," she said as she took off her coat.
I didn't answer. I didn't want to imagine what she looked like in a coffin.
"She wears a white gown, and her hands are folded in a rosary. She looks so peaceful," Oma said.
I was scared and mad.
"I don't want to see her," I said suddenly.
Oma looked at me for a moment and went into the hallway to hang up her coat. She took a long time, carefully arranging the other coats on the rack.
I was holding my head in my hands, staring ahead: Oma went out to see Mom and I didn't. The thought kept repeating itself. Oma was talking to me when she came back into the living room.
"August, are you listening?"
"What?"
"Are you OK?" Oma asked.
"I don't want to see her!"
"I understand. Maybe tomorrow," she tried.
"No. Never."
I got up to go to my room.
"Leave me alone, just leave me alone," I whispered to myself, as I raced up the small stairway.

    On Wednesday, I stood in front of the window. The church bells were ringing for the funeral. My grandparents' home was comfortable and warm. Someone had lit a special candle for me. I had the chess game from Uncle Louis' house in my hands. It would be quiet at home for a while. I could play for several hours. I turned away from the window, and put my game on the table. As I moved the small plastic pieces randomly around on the board, I tried to picture the people I knew at the funeral. Dad, Hugo, Aunt Fie, Aunt Netty, Oma and Opa. I wondered who would be crying. Finally, I dozed off, surrounded by tiny pawns and rooks.

I woke up suddenly when the front door opened. The people returning from the funeral talked loudly. The ceremony was over and the drinks at the funeral home after the burial had loosened the serious mood. I heard laughter as people took off their coats in the hallway. Dad was not laughing. He looked intensely serious and did not say much. We had not talked since Sunday.

I was mad at him for not telling me that Mom had died. I avoided him.

"August, it was a beautiful ceremony," he said.

I didn't answer.

Bottles of sherry and genever gin were opened and Camel cigarettes were brought in. Soon, everybody had full glasses. A blue fog of cigarette smoke filled the small living room. My aunts and Oma were busy talking to their visitors. Hugo and I were quietly sitting in a corner. I wanted to go home.

Half an hour later, Uncle Louis arrived to pick us up. Without coming into the house, he waved from his car. Dad got up and said a short goodbye to the guests, thanking them for coming to the funeral. It was quiet for a moment, but the busy chatting had started again as we were picking up our coats in the hallway and heading out the front door.

13

At Home

After the funeral, I stayed home from school for a week. It felt like vacation but I knew it wasn't because my classmates were in school. Dad was quiet and hardly talked to me. He was upstairs a lot. I was still mad at him for not telling me about Mom.

When I went back to school I felt as if all the attention was on me. The classroom was silent. Everybody knew about me but nobody said anything. The teacher started class promptly at 8:30. Hugo was also back in school, and Dad was working in the dark room: we all started again.

I worked hard at school. I had more time for homework because my friends weren't visiting as often. Dad did not want kids running around in the house, and my friends were less eager to visit. Arie, who never kept his mouth shut, told me why he was not visiting anymore.
"My Mom does not want me to visit you anymore," he said.
"Why?"
"She said that there is no Mom to take care of things in your house anymore." Arie sounded matter-of-fact about it. He believed his Mom.
"Does it matter that it's only my dad at home?" I asked.
"I don't know. I just know I shouldn't see you at your house anymore. You're welcome to visit us." He made it sound like a handout.

"No thanks. See you around, Arie."
I turned around and walked away. I wouldn't visit Arie anymore.

      One month after Mom's death, on a Saturday afternoon, the weather was windy and chilly. Dad was upstairs, fixing wiring in the dark room. Hugo and I were playing a game of Stratego in the living room.
"Hugo, where did you go after the hospital?" I asked.
He looked at me.
"Do you really want to talk about that now?" He was surprised.
"Yes, I do," I said quietly.
"OK, OK. Let's forget about the game."
He turned around, putting one hand on his forehead, staring out the window.
"After you left the Emergency Room…."
He paused.
"…the priest finished the Last Rites. The doctor told us that Mom needed to go to Utrecht. He asked if Dad was going with the ambulance.
Dad immediately looked at me. Then he bent over, and whispered to me that I should go instead. 'That's fine,' I said."
Hugo was still staring out the window.
"What a deal," he mumbled quietly.
"Why didn't you say no?" I asked.
"Dad was too nervous. He'd panic. I knew it."
It was raining heavily now and sudden gusts clattered against the windows.
I was afraid to find out about the ambulance ride but I was curious too.
"How was the ride?" I asked.
"The two ambulance people sat in the front of the small Volkswagen bus. It was narrow in the back so I was close to Mom's face. She looked at me, turning away only as her breathing became difficult. She didn't say anything. I tried to talk to her but I don't think she was listening. The sirens were loud and the blue emergency light reflected in the windows of houses as we drove by. We arrived at the Lek ferry and discovered there was no service on Sunday before noon. I heard the driver swear to his mate in the front. We had to take the bridge 10 miles down the river, losing a half an hour.
It started pouring just before we reached Utrecht and we slowed down. Still, twice we almost got into an accident in the city.

When we arrived at the hospital, Mom asked softly 'Are they going to take care of me now? Are they going to take care of me now?' I told her they would and put my hand on her forehead. The backdoor opened and they took her into the hospital."

Hugo was done. I didn't know what to say.

"God, I hated these sirens! They were loud," Hugo said.

He got up and left. Alone in the room, I could see Mom's eyes in the emergency room. Hugo and I never talked about the ambulance ride again.

14

Remembrance Mass

We rose from our pews.
We believe in one God, the Father, the Almighty, maker of heaven and earth, of all that is seen and unseen.

I whispered the words from the Mass book.

We believe in one Lord, Jesus Christ, the only Son of God, eternally begotten of the Father, God from God, Light from Light, true God from true God, begotten not made, one in Being with the Father. Through him all things were made. For us men and for our salvation he came down from heaven.

I glanced at Oma. The tips of her mouth were down. She looked like that when she was tense. Oma knew the Creed by heart, easily following the priest's words.

… by the power of the Holy Spirit he was born of the Virgin Mary, and became man.

I didn't understand this part.

For our sake he was crucified under Pontius Pilate; he suffered, died, and was buried. On the third day he rose again in fulfillment of the Scriptures; he ascended into heaven and is seated at the right hand of the Father. He will come again in glory to judge the living and the dead, and his kingdom will have no end.

I was looking at the small statue near the pillar next to me; Oma nudged me to look ahead. She looked at me sternly.

We believe in the Holy Spirit, the Lord, the giver of life, who proceeds from the Father and the Son. With the Father and the Son he is worshipped and glorified. He has spoken through the Prophets. We believe in one holy catholic and apostolic Church. We acknowledge one baptism for the forgiveness of our sins. We look for the resurrection of the dead, and the life of the world to come. Amen.

We had reached the part where they said Mom's name. First the sick people, sometimes a long list of more than ten names. Then the priest said: "This Mass is dedicated to the memory of Maria Hendrika Wilhelmina Brouwers."

Oma was always relieved when she heard Mom's name. We paid for the special 'remembrance' Mass and sometimes the priest forgot to mention Mom. As we were leaving church Oma told me that it had been a beautiful Mass. At the back of the church I lit a candle in Mom's memory. Aunt Netty paid for the candle.

15

The Sounds Of Spoons

After Mom's death my father put an ad in the newspaper for a housekeeper. Monique responded and got the job. She was nineteen and good-looking with a friendly round face. Her cheeks were shiny and she had a hearty laugh. Monique was getting married soon and spent hours reading about marriage in a book she had found in our house.

When Oma visited, she made comments to Dad about the long time Monique was spending reading and not working. Dad seemed unconcerned. "She is just a young girl who is engaged," he said. Hugo and I believed that he was afraid to tell her to work and not to read. Dad did not want to have to place a new ad.

To me, Monique was an intruder. She was there because my mother was dead. I was not going to let her forget that. Day after day, I noticed her incessant reading and felt angry. At lunch one day, Dad made a compliment about Monique's work. I got up and walked to the breakfront in the living room – the same one my mom had so desperately coveted and then so desperately hated once we bought it.

"You call this good work!" I said, stroking dust from the glass plate. There was a lot of dust.

It was silent for a moment, then Dad said with a low, serious, voice: "August, you should not say things like that!"

Monique got up, putting her face in her hands, and left the room in tears. My father followed her to the foyer. He tried to talk to her into staying, but she left and never came back.

For a while, Dad did not advertise. But within weeks, the house became messy and Dad was again trying to get help. He also wanted the companionship, I sensed. He needed help to handle the stress of raising two children. Dad routinely threatened Hugo and me that he would send us to an orphanage if we did not behave better.

"This can't go on any longer. I guess we can't stay together like this!" he would say in his abrupt, agitated way.

I worried about the possible breakup. Hugo seemed less concerned. He felt bad for me but knew that he could leave home in a year and a half for college.

Before Mom became ill, Hugo and I went to church with Mom every week. Dad always stayed home. He did not like the crowds in church and he would pray at home, he said. He also claimed to have a special dispensation from the Church. When Mom became ill, Hugo and I went to church by ourselves. We maintained our Sunday routine until Mom died. After her death, our churchgoing days ended. Dad did not seem to mind. Sundays became free days and I looked forward to listening to the afternoon soccer reports on the radio.

Dad was busier than ever in his photo developing business. Hugo and I helped out, drying pictures and sorting them for fifty cents an hour. My father spent hour after hour in the dark room upstairs, often until midnight. Sometimes, he lost his cool, taking his anger out on the neighbors, the Mandos family. He would yell loudly that they were spying on him. Or, that they were following him every time he went on the stairs. He especially hated Mrs. Mandos.

"That woman is just like the devil!" he would say in an enraged voice.

The next round of housekeeper ads delivered quick results. The lady from Groningen was taller than my father, and wore big, old-fashioned glasses with transparent frames. She had a strong Northern accent, cutting off the n's at the end of every word. It sounded strange and ugly to us. She had a thin nose and a small round mouth. Her hair was mostly gray. She looked old.

After her first week, I fell ill with a fever. She told me that she needed to take my temperature rectally. My mother and my aunts had always taken my temperature under my armpit. She began by pushing me on my stomach but I resisted. Then we started to wrestle for control of my body. She was strong and finally forced me onto my stomach. I was crying and moving wildly, but somehow she managed to insert the thermometer. She sighed contentedly. I hated her guts.

The next day I started my boycott. I did not talk to her unless I absolutely needed to. I was as unfriendly as possible. After a week, my father told her to leave.

Angry about the noises next door, my father began slamming the darkroom door. Hugo and I would sit in the living room, hoping for the noises to stop. As Dad continued to madly bang the door I asked Hugo if we could leave the house. We would stroll along the Westersingel canal, nervous about the loud noises at home. Hugo and I would stay away for an hour before going back home. We would carefully open the door, listening for sounds. If everything was quiet we would go in.

Hugo cooked, did grocery shopping and helped in Dad's business when it was busy. Three months after Mom died, Hugo received his Easter report card. It was dismal and, without improvement, he was not going to be promoted to the final year of high school.
The June day Hugo received his final report card I waited in the driveway for him.
I saw him on his bike and I shouted: "Did you make it?!"
He did not respond as he solemnly parked his bike.
As he walked past me, he said softly: "I guess I'll just have to do it over again."
I raced into the house and told Dad: "Hugo did not make it!"
My father looked very disappointed. He had written to the school's principal asking for leniency due to our family circumstances.

Hugo came into the house and Dad verified the news with him. It was quiet. Dad went into the kitchen. I didn't know how to cheer up Hugo so I followed Dad, who started to somberly grind coffee. Then Hugo entered the kitchen, holding his report card in front of him.
He had passed!

My father had the biggest smile I had ever seen. With a laugh, he said: "Hugo, you should not joke about these things."
It was the happiest lunch of the year.

Dad didn't feel comfortable speaking about Mom except in general, abstract terms.
"She was a very good woman. She is with angels now."
He didn't like private, risky topics. He simply shut down, putting up a safety shield. If Hugo and I pushed too long he became angry, and would tell us he had his own privacy which we should respect. Often, Dad just stalked off, avoiding confrontation. He hated to be reminded of the bad things that happened. He never raised the topic. It became taboo inside our home. From the outside, our family must have looked just fine. Dad was the hard-working widower who had two nice boys. Dad liked it that way. He did not want too many people asking questions.

Dad placed another advertisement at the end of that first summer. He received one reaction. The lady from Enkhuizen visited on a Sunday afternoon. She was pretty and had dark hair. She reminded me of Mom. Dad asked me to come into the salon to meet her. She was friendly and I liked her. How was Dad able to land such a find? He seemed very positive too. In the next few days the two were on the phone a lot and Dad was cheerful. She was asking many questions about the past and, surprisingly, my father did not seem to mind talking about it.

Two weeks later, she called to tell him that she was no longer interested. My father was floored. He called his sister Toos, complaining about his bad luck. Several days later, Aunt Toos called back. She found out that the lady from Enkhuizen was a novelist who must have been looking for material for a new book. One year later, the Lady from Enkhuizen wrote a book featuring a widower with two boys.

One day, Dad was slamming doors again. Hugo and I were in the living room. This time Dad rushed down the stairs. He was in a rage, stomping his feet on the stairs. I was so scared I felt a lump in my throat and my legs were trembling. Hugo and I rushed to meet Dad at the bottom of the stairs. He brusquely moved past us, pacing back and forth in the foyer. He was agitated, short of breath.

"I'll get them, I'll get them!" he yelled frantically.
Hugo followed closely behind him.
I wanted to stop Dad and felt myself getting mad at him. I grunted an angry sound, getting a step closer to him.
"August, no!" Hugo said.
I stepped back, trembling.

Dad went into the living room and picked up the small typewriter I used for writing notes. He lifted it high and threw it on the floor with a terrific bang. Then he stepped on it, cracking the typewriter's metal letter arms. He paused for a second and turned to the glass doors to the backyard. Before my dad had the chance to open them, Hugo put his arms around Dad's neck. My father struggled but Hugo managed to hold him.

Finally, Dad gave up, breaking down and nervously crying. It was over. We didn't say anything. Dad left the room and went back upstairs to his dark room.
At dinner, you could only hear the sounds of spoons on the soup plates.

In November, eleven months after my mom died, Dad placed one more ad for a housekeeper. Again, he got just one response, this one from a lady from Delft. She was unable to use one leg and her head bobbed up and down as she walked. Her name was Leah. She was very sweet to me but I could not get used to her stiff leg and her bobbing head.
My father urged us to be nice to Leah. She called one night when we were watching TV, and Hugo and I could follow our dad chatting on the phone with her. After a while, Dad did not know what to say to her. In despair, he started to describe a TV commercial for a vacuum cleaner to her. "Oh Leah, you should see this vacuum: it turns around!" Hugo and I looked at each other, rolling our eyes.

Weeks passed, and she called often. One night, my brother told me he heard that they were planning to get married.
"Don't we have anything to say about it?" I asked him angrily.
"Doesn't matter!" He believed it was a done deal.
I thought about Mom and didn't want my father to get married, not to Leah or anyone else for that matter.
A week later, Leah was involved in a serious car accident. She needed to stay in the hospital for several weeks. One day, she called from the hospital and cancelled the wedding plans. She must have had doubts about Dad's commitment. Dad did not appear to be sad about it. He must have had his own doubts.

We never saw Leah again.

Dad's attempts to find a housekeeper were over. I wasn't ready for one. Titia, a toothless woman who drove a motorcycle, came by every Tuesday and Thursday to clean our house and do the laundry.
That was all I could handle.

16

The Trip To Italy

In the summer after Mom died, I went on a vacation to Italy with Aunt Netty and Aunt Fie. My mom's sisters wanted to do something special for me. It was the first time that I ever left Holland.
    We traveled by train on the day of the 1966 World Cup soccer final. I had followed the tournament very closely -- I didn't miss a game on TV -- and the thought of not seeing the final game put a damper on my excitement. Our International D-train was different from Dutch trains. It had separate compartments for six people and a narrow aisle outside the compartments allowed us to walk through the train. On one of our first on-board excursions, we visited the train's dining car. The tables were covered with neat white cloths, and the extra wide windows offered spectacular views of the countryside. A waiter took our orders for dinner. It seemed that my aunts were used to this. They had traveled a lot, even by airplane.
When we got close to Switzerland, a man came into our compartment.
"You can see the mountains!" he said.
Quickly, I moved into the aisle and stretched to look ahead. I had never seen anything like it. Holland was flat, particularly where I lived in the area between the big rivers. Here, colossal pieces of rock stretched for miles and miles, as far as the eye could see. I tilted my head to see the snow-covered mountain tops. After a half an hour, Aunt Netty told me to come back

into our compartment. "You are too young to be standing there all the time!" she said. The people on the train smoked cigarettes that smelled different than Dad's tobacco. They spoke a different language.

At the first dinner in the hotel, the manager came to our table to welcome us to Celle Ligure, Italy. When my aunts told him that I was a soccer fan and had missed seeing the World Cup final he said: "It was one of the greatest finals ever. The English beat the Germans 4-2 in overtime. You really missed something!" My aunts tried hard to console me but I felt homesick already.

Eurotex, a travel agency in Rotterdam, organized our trip to Italy. Armando, Eurotex's Italian agent, took care of us in the hotel. We nicknamed Armando 'Little Almond' because he was short and had a dark complexion. He talked a lot but did very little. Armando was transfixed by Aunt Fie, whose blond hair had not escaped his attention. Italian men like blondes because it's an unusual color for them. My aunts told me that.
In our first week, Aunt Fie got a bad cold and the fever kept her in bed. After one day, my aunts decided to call the doctor. Armando was our intermediary.
"No problem. We'll get a doctor for Miss Sophia right away."
He meant business. Less than forty minutes had passed when Armando knocked on Aunt Fie's door. He was alone and circled the bed casting his eyes on my aunt, who was sitting upright in her bed wearing her pajamas.
"The doctor will be here any minute. Don't worry."
He stood firmly near the balcony window staring at Aunt Fie's breasts. Aunt Fie pulled the sheets up a bit more and looked at Aunt Netty and me.
"You guys stay right here," she said firmly.
Of course, we did not move. We were her sentries now.
"Oh, Miss Sophia! No need for that. The doctor will be here any minute. Don't worry," Armando declared. There was no answer and nobody moved.

Five minutes later the doctor arrived. He asked to see the patient alone. Armando was now near the balcony door. He stayed put. Did he not hear the doctor's request? He turned around and started a barrage of Italian words directed at the doctor. The astonished doctor responded briefly. In Italian. Armando started to talk even faster, and he seemed to be

pleading. Suddenly, Aunt Fie looked at him and said firmly "No!"
"*Si senora, naturalemente*," Armando said meekly. And then in a louder voice to us: "The doctor wants to see Miss Sophia alone. We must leave now."
Afterwards, Aunt Fie complained about the doctor's lengthy exam of her breasts.

I returned to Culemborg, tanned, and still impressed by the mountains and hills I had seen in Switzerland and Italy. Suddenly, Culemborg did not look the same anymore. Or Holland for that matter. Everything was so flat, the beaches small and chilly, the people quiet, mostly staring at each other on buses, trains, and in waiting rooms. I had liked being in another country. My Dad was surprised.
"You weren't homesick, August?"
"No, Dad. The two weeks were over before I knew it. I loved swimming in the Mediterranean Sea. And the food in the hotel was very good."
"It was very special you went to Italy, August."
"Yes, Dad. I know."
Dad had only been to Germany and Switzerland during his lifetime. He had to get used to the fact that his 10-year old son had just gone further afield than he had ever been.
"Are you happy to be back?" he asked tentatively.
"Sure. I like to play in the backyard in the summer."
"I'll get lunch ready in a minute," Dad said.
He sat down in his chair, taking out his tobacco box. Within seconds, he rolled his cigarette and the familiar heavy tobacco smell was everywhere.

17

Moving On

On a sunny day in June of 1967 I was running home, turning into the path to our garage. From the back porch, I could see Hugo in the living room, sitting close to the radio. His right ear was touching the speaker.
"There is war!" he cried through the open double doors. Israel had attacked Egypt and destroyed its planes. The announcer read off the countries that had declared war on Israel. The list went on and on: Syria, Jordan, Saudi Arabia, United Emirates, and, of course, Egypt.
"Nasser is a dangerous man," Dad said at lunch. "The Jews are going to take all of Jerusalem and they will never give it away again."
He referred to the Jews as 'the chosen people' and the people with the oldest faith. At least in this respect he had outgrown his Roman Catholic education which had taught him that the Jews were guilty of crucifying Jesus. It must have been World War II. Israel was held in the highest regard by Dad.
My brother and I followed the news closely in the next several days.
It was our first war. It sounded like a soccer game: victories, offensive, surprise attack, and reserves. Israel easily won.

One night, Dad was working upstairs. Hugo seemed a bit nervous when he turned on the TV at seven to watch the network program.

"August, watch this," he urged.

I wanted to play outside but Hugo insisted and I sat down in front of the TV. It was a boring show. In the middle of the program the screen went totally white and for a few seconds nothing happened. I looked at Hugo but he was mesmerized by the screen. Then, from the left, a woman with long hair walked slowly into view. She was nude. We both took a good look, getting closer to the TV: she was nude. The woman disappeared in less than five seconds.

I was stunned. I had never seen anything like it.

Hugo turned off the TV, and looked at me with curiosity.

"What do you know about sex?" he asked.

He said it in a worried tone. My dad had never talked to me about sex. I tried to answer because I didn't want to look dumb in front of Hugo. But it was clear that I did not know much. We went into the kitchen and Hugo started an expose about copulation and what it meant. He had just been reading a book about these things. I had seen the book once or twice, but he had been carefully hiding it, from me and from Dad.

I listened intently to my learned brother.

When he was done, I had my questions ready.

"How long does it take?"

"It can be as short as five minutes but when people just get married they can do it the whole night," he said with authority.

"Do you need to have all your clothes off to do it?" I was still thinking about the nude woman on TV.

"No, you can do it with almost all your clothes on. It's just easier to take your clothes off."

Dad was coming down the stairway.

"Let's stop here, August. I think this is enough for tonight," Hugo said.

Before Dad was downstairs we returned to watching TV, but I was too excited to pay attention. Dad did not have a clue what we had been talking about.

Hugo put me to bed every night. He told a story and kissed me goodnight. If Dad had one of his rages, bamming doors upstairs, we would go to bed at the same time and Hugo tried to soothe my fears.

"Hugo, what happens if we go to an orphanage? Do we stay together?"
"August, Dad is just talking. We'll never go to an orphanage."
"Why does he keep on talking about it?" I asked.
"Because he sometimes loses his cool. Don't worry. We'll stay together." He seemed to know what he was talking about.

One night -- he was already in college -- Hugo came home late from a trip to France. He came to my bedside and, while I was sound asleep, whispered a story into my ears. It repeated itself:

> *"It was night, a very dark night*
> *And the crows were pooping on the windows of the high houses,*
> *And under a tree there were seven thieves,*
> *And the leader of the thieves said:*
> *'Pedro, tell me a story that will really scare me!'*
> *And Pedro began:*
> *'It was night, a very dark night,*
> *And the crows ,etc.'* "

The next morning, I woke up vaguely remembering that I had been laughing hard and loud in my bed but Hugo told me that I never woke up. He was funny with his pranks.

I visited the cemetery in Tiel as often as I could. I now felt guilty for not going to the funeral. At the train station, I would buy fresh cut flowers and lean them against the handle bars of my bike. At the cemetery I went to the area in the back where the vases were kept and selected the nicest one I could find. I used the old water pump to get fresh water in the vase, saying hello to other people who were putting flowers on graves.
I always needed to talk to Mom when I stood in front of her grave. A prayer was not enough. I needed to tell her about what was happening to me. How school was going and how Dad was going nuts sometimes. How Hugo and I talked a lot. I cleaned up mud on the grave after a rain shower. In the spring and fall, Aunt Netty and Aunt Fie planted flowers on the grave. The flowers looked very nice, and even Dad said a good word about my aunts. Afterwards, I'd go to my grandparents' grave to pray one Our Father. I always thought of Father Stricker

when I did this. He had me do more Hail Mary's for my sins, but now I could write my own ticket, praying for Oma and Opa Swanenberg.

The cemetery was beautiful in the summer. The trees were filled with birds and you could hear them clearly because the cemetery was so quiet. Some branches were low enough that you had to duck to get to the grave.

Dad's design of the gravestone was simple but beautiful. It was symmetric with Mom's name on one side. It felt as if the other half -- where Dad's name would go some day -- just needed filling out. I did not want to be in Dad's shoes. Each time he saw the gravestone he must have thought that it was just a matter of time. He was very serious at the cemetery, the edges of his mouth turned down in his customary sad way. He always seemed touched by his parents' grave. After a short prayer, Dad would leave in an abrupt fashion. He never wanted to stop at the World War II grave and monument. He had had enough and wanted to get out. Hugo and I tried to keep up as he left the cemetery.

When I was on my own, I often stopped at the long gray monument for the fourteen people who were shot by the Germans in 1944. They were in the liberated town of Wamel, just across the river Waal. The Germans were able to capture them because the Canadians had left their positions to support the attack on the Waal bridges at Nijmegen. The prisoners were taken to Tiel and summarily shot the next day. Their collective grave was the largest at Tiel's cemetery.

I felt sad as I left. The loud grinding sound of the pebbles on the path gave me a headache. I grabbed my bike and quickly left the cemetery area.

I knew I would be back.

Three years after Mom died, Aunt Fie married Uncle Aart, who was a fruit trader. Oma was unhappy at first because Uncle Aart was divorced with a son and daughter from his first marriage. Uncle Aart grew up in Leerbroek, a strongly Dutch Reformed area. There was no church wedding. Aunt Fie wore white but didn't have a train on her dress.

Even Dad attended the wedding. He didn't like Aunt Fie because she could be outspoken, especially about Dad. But on the wedding day Dad drank his gin at the reception and for two hours it seemed as if everything had been forgiven. Dad talked to Aunt Netty and other members of the Brouwers family. The reception was animated and there was lots of laughter. Hugo and I proudly received compliments for our new sports jackets. Waiters moved around from table to table offering wine from a serving tray. I drank two glasses of wine. Hugo stopped me when I tried to take a third glass. He kept close tabs on me that afternoon.

Dad was already tipsy from too many gins, joking and laughing with people he couldn't stand.

18

The New School

Dad hated the house in Culemborg. It was filled with bad memories. He dreaded going into the cellar where my mother had grabbed the bottle of photo developing acid. He couldn't stand the bedroom because it reminded him of the many hours he spent awake with Mom. When the opportunity came to move back to Tiel, he seized it. Dad and I -- Hugo was away at college -- settled into a modest two-bedroom apartment on the outskirts of town.

In September 1969, I transferred from Culemborg's high school to Linge High School at Tiel. Dad worried about my being the youngest in my class. When I had stomach aches in first grade as a six-year old, the doctor told my parents that I was probably nervous about being the youngest student. My stomach aches disappeared after one year but my dad never forgot what the doctor had said. He continued to worry, despite my good grades.

Mr. Cevaal, my math teacher in Tiel, gave Dad new reasons for his worries. Mr. Cevaal was a tall man, with a nearly bald head and a pair of heavy glasses. His voice was deep and strong, commanding immediate respect. When he entered the classroom, his students became silent, a rare achievement at Linge High School. After sitting down in his chair, Mr. Cevaal's first action each day was to neatly organize his papers before calling his class to order. He was an engineer by training, a precise man. On the first day of classes, the new name on his list caught his attention.

"August, now that is a special name!" he said.

Some students started to giggle. I was surprised and embarrassed. At my old school, nobody giggled about my name.

"What Algebra-I topics were covered at your old school, August?" Mr. Cevaal asked after the giggles subsided.

Nervously, I mentioned some of the topics we covered last year. Mr. Cevaal seemed impressed. My jitters started to slowly disappear as he declared:

"You are well ahead of the students here. You should not have any problems."

Had this stern man just declared me a prodigy? Did the class think a new math genius had arrived? Immediately, I received lots of attention from the established wizards. Here was a person who could not be denied.

Four weeks later, the first big Algebra exam took place. It was harder than I expected but I believed I had done well enough. Two days later I was nervously hoping for the best when Mr. Cevaal's verdict came:

"And here we have August's work; we had expected this exam would be easy for him but he received a 3+ grade."

The class fell silent. I felt my breath taken away. My teacher's single line of commentary cut deeply. On a scale of 1 to 10, I had missed the minimal passing grade of 6 by half! The "+" was a sinister footnote to the disaster. Instantly, I became afraid of math and this big man.

"August, please come to the blackboard. Here's your chance to make up for this exam by doing today's assignment," he demanded. This was the ultimate punishment. My knees were shaking as I approached the board. I had done my homework but I was not allowed to use my notes. Mr. Cevaal wanted students to show their comprehension. My shaking became worse as I stood in front of the class. I had trouble writing down the exercise, let alone solving the problem. Mr. Cevaal gave me less than thirty seconds.

"August, you can sit down now," he said impatiently.

He immediately called on one of the math wizards who easily completed the exercise. In less than a minute I had gone from genius to dunce.

I had a tough time with mathematics that year. My grades were lower than they had ever been, and there was a moment that my advancement to the next grade was in jeopardy. At year's end, I secured advancement by promising to Mr. Cevaal that I would not take Algebra the next year.

Mr. Cevaal's last class of the year consisted of a student-by-student discussion of next year's classes. When he got to my name, he leaned against my side of the two-person bench and faced me.

"August, you are making a good decision to take Algebra out of your schedule for next year. Lots of luck in your new program."

He sounded gracious and merciful. It was over. I would not have to see the man again.

I never talked to Mr. Cevaal again. Years later, I received a Master's degree, with highest honors, in mathematical economics from a Dutch University and proceeded to study applied mathematics at graduate school in the United States.

Mr. Cevaal would have asked me to come to the blackboard to prove it

After we had moved to Tiel, Dad's violent outbursts stopped. Still, it was hard to handle his moodiness, which sometimes led to tense, completely silent meals at home. Often, I went over to Oma and Opa for lunch. The conversations were livelier and happy. I enjoyed going there but I felt bad leaving Dad alone.

One day at lunch, five years after Mom died, I asked Oma to tell me about my mom.

"What do you want to know, August?" she asked.

"I want to know about the time when Mom was a child."

"Well, let's see…" Oma poured another cup of tea.

"August, you know that my dad was a captain on a river boat?" she asked.

I nodded.

"In November of 1927, we went for new supplies to Belgium. First Antwerp, then Brussels. I was more than eight months pregnant with your mother. I had hoped that my dad could leave for Rotterdam quickly, so I'd have the baby in the Netherlands but the supplies were delayed and Riny was born in Elsene, a small town near Brussels."

Oma had taken her glasses off and was looking out the back window.

"Did she get a Belgian passport, Oma?"
"No, no. She was Dutch, of course."
"Did Mom like school, Oma?"
"Your Mom was very good at school. She always had good grades. I was very proud of her."
Suddenly, Oma sounded more serious.
"Riny was well liked by her teachers. A lot of her grade school friends went to college preparatory schools. We sent her to the vocational school. That's where working people like us would send their kids. Anyway, she got a fine secretarial job with her vocational degree. She worked in Geldermalsen at the Chamotte Union factory and did well."
"What did she do there?"
"She typed letters and arranged appointments for the men that were running the factory. They told your Mom that her foreign languages were excellent and that she was very quick in shorthand writing."
Oma got up and picked up her tea. She went into the kitchen and got set to do the dishes.
"Oma, can I help dry the dishes?" I was curious to hear more about Mom.
"Of course," Oma said, surprised.
"How did Mom and Dad meet?"
"Your Aunt Toos was Riny's best friend. Although Toos went to the Gymnasium, she and Riny kept in touch. Riny met your Dad through Toos. They got married the year before your brother was born."
"Oma, why did Mom not wear a white dress at her wedding?"
Oma, accidentally splashing dishwater on the floor, looked at me briefly and then turned her head, away from me.
"Well, August...."
She paused.
"Hugo was born a little earlier than expected and your Mom and Dad didn't have much time to prepare a large wedding," she said quietly.
Her tone had changed, as if she was now speaking to herself. She did not seem to want to talk with me anymore.
I finished drying off one more plate and threw the dish towel on the table.
"Oma, I'm gonna be in the backyard now!" I exclaimed.
"That's fine, August. Have fun."

The moment Oma started to talk about Dad her voice changed. I sensed that she hated him for what he did to her daughter.

I didn't feel comfortable around girls in high school. Most girls wore fashionable mini-skirts and I loved to watch them when they walked by seductively. But I got nervous when I talked to them, and didn't want to get too close. I envied the boys who had no trouble asking girls out or walking with them during recess, holding hands and kissing in the alley behind school.
I often complained to Dad about my awkwardness.
"I'll never get a girlfriend, I just know it," I said.
"Oh August, that's nonsense. Of course you'll find a girl."
After a pause, Dad would continue in his own poetic mood, using his best English and German.
"Somehow, somewhere. *Irgendwo, irgendwann.*"
He was much more convinced than I was. He didn't know how hard it was for me.

At the yearly school party, I wanted to dance with a pretty classmate but I didn't have the courage to ask her. She was popular, and constantly surrounded by a circle of friends. When I arrived home at 2:30 a.m., I had had too many beers and I got sick to my stomach, waking up Dad. He had been worried about me. The next day was my birthday but I was too sick to get out of bed. When Uncle Aart and Aunt Fie visited for my birthday they knew I had been drinking too much. Uncle Aart laughed about it; he seemed to understand.
If I found a girlfriend I could never ask her to visit my house. Dad had caused an ugly spectacle when Hugo first came home with a girl. I didn't want that to happen to me. Dad might be reciting poetic German words to me, but he was happy that I remained firmly attached to home without a girlfriend.

I wrote poems every night, carefully typing them on the large Remington Dad used for his business. I loved typing short poems on small pieces of paper. Sometimes I wrote dreamily about untouchable, beautiful girls, but often my words were harsh, negative and hopeless. I felt angry, mostly because I was in some kind of prison with Dad, who only went out twice a year when we visited Aunt Toos for Easter and Christmas. I couldn't talk about it with anybody because I felt I would be betraying Dad if I told Oma or one of my aunts. Dad was so negative about the Brouwers family that he made me feel guilty about visiting any of them. I was envious of Hugo who was out of the house and stayed out, and took as much distance as possible from my dad.

Once, in the fall of 1971, Hugo stopped by unexpectedly. It was Tuesday and he happened to be in the Tiel area. When he was about to leave he took me aside.
"August, do you really know enough about sex?"
He looked intense and serious.
"Sure," I said as convincingly as possible.
"I am asking you because I know that Dad won't talk about it. Are you sure you know what it's all about?"
I had no clue. I did not know much more beyond the discussion with Hugo two years before, when the nude lady was on TV. I knew I'd only embarrass myself by asking something.
"Hugo, I'm fine. Don't worry."
He looked at me for a split second, in doubt.
"OK. I'm off."
Hugo was going back to his college studies in Utrecht. To me it seemed like the promised land.
As I waved goodbye, I wondered what things I didn't know about sex.

I had started to like rock music. I used to listen mostly to Beethoven and Chopin because of Dad, but I had my own record player now. I discovered a song by Jefferson Airplane that I loved. It was called 'White Rabbit.'
The lead guitar had a dream-like opening and the drums played this great background rhythm which became ever stronger. Grace Slick's words were powerful and haunting, building to the climactic end: "Feed your head. Feed your head."
The song was short and I played it again and again.

One pill makes you larger
And one pill makes you small,
And the ones that mother gives you
Don't do anything at all.
Go ask Alice
When she's ten feet tall.
And if you go chasing rabbits
And you know you're going to fall,
Tell 'em a hookah smoking caterpillar

*Has given you the call.
Call Alice
When she was just small.
When the men on the chessboard
Get up and tell you where to go
And you've just had some kind of mushroom
And your mind is moving low.
Go ask Alice
I think she'll know.
When logic and proportion
Have fallen sloppy dead,
And the White Knight is talking backwards,
And the Red Queen's 'off with her head!'
Remember what the dormouse said:
'Feed your head. Feed your head.'*

    The strong, haunting voice made me think of Mom. It always sounded like she was telling me something in 'White Rabbit.'

19

Final Exam

Saturday, June 3, 1972 was a warm, humid day. I was dressed up in my blue jacket for the final day of high school exams and I felt hot. My history oral exam in the morning was my last test. The exam would take 20 minutes. Some of my schoolmates were already done. I was envious, worrying about blowing it and not graduating.

As I walked into the exam room my history teacher was smoking a cigarette. He was short and completely bald. I noticed his trembling hand as he tipped the ashes off the cigarette with a quick move. Seeing that made me less nervous. A large man with heavy-set glasses was sitting next to him. He seemed at ease. My teacher introduced him, but I immediately forgot his name. He was the Committee representative, mandated by government to ensure an objective oral exam. I did not see him before at my other orals and I hoped he would not be asking most questions.

The first question was about the origins of World War I. I began to answer. After about a minute, I saw the Committee representative nod, and my teacher was no longer nervously smiling. I continued with Sarajevo, August 1914, The Russians, The Germans, The French, Ypres, Verdun, The Americans, and finally Versailles. I paused, almost ten minutes had passed. My teacher wanted to start a new question but the Committee representative interrupted.
"That's enough. I've heard enough," he said decisively.

"What is your major in college going to be?" he continued.
"Economics, sir," I responded.
"Are you sure? As a matter of practice, I never make comments during an exam, but I strongly urge you to reconsider. History would be a great choice for you."
My teacher turned red. From pride.
I did not know what to do with the comments.
"I think I'll stick to economics," I answered. "Everybody has told me you could get a good job that way."
"Think about it. You still have time."
The exam was over. I received a perfect score of 100.
At the graduation ceremonies later that day it turned out I was ranked top in the class. Marja, a girl who ranked second, burst into tears at the news. She couldn't stand me.
The committee agent congratulated me. "You will have a great future," he said with pride.
I was still glowing, coming down the stairs, when I saw Aunt Fie in the crowd.
"I am the number one graduate!" I exclaimed.
"Congratulations, that's wonderful!" she exclaimed.
Hugo wasn't there because he had a big exam on Monday.
As usual, Dad did not come to the ceremony. He was expecting me to come home as soon as possible. To celebrate.

  At home, thirty minutes later, Dad uncorked a sherry bottle. He looked happy and was very proud of my high grades. I felt strange that we were the only two celebrating, but I knew that Aunt Fie and Aunt Netty, who were at the ceremony, were not welcome in our home. Dad couldn't stand them and the feeling was mutual. I told Dad that I was planning to visit my friend Paul's home later. Afterwards, Paul and I would go to people's homes for various parties around town. I wouldn't be back early.
"That's fine, August. I just want you to stay here for a while. I didn't get this bottle for nothing." It almost sounded like an order.
Of course, he didn't get the bottle himself. I had bought it the day before at the grocery store.
I wanted to ask him what he meant by 'a while' but decided against it.
Dad poured two glasses with sherry and we said cheers.
"Your mother would be so proud of you now. If only she could be here," Dad said in a serious way.

He always became sentimental on occasions like this. I hated it. He had not mentioned Mom in a long time and even now he didn't say anything more. She had been dead six years already. I quickly drank my glass of sherry. I had parties to go to. I couldn't wait for college to start so I could be on my own.

20

College

Dad lived alone in his Tiel apartment after I left for college. During my first year in college he retired from his photography business with a small pension. He painted during the day. The serious, allegorical pictures from the past made way for more playful topics. A winter landscape, a boat under a tree, a tent encampment, and water cascades were all far removed from the 19th Century neo-romantic mythology subjects we had grown up with. He simply seemed to have more fun painting in his free time.

Unfortunately, he decided on a unique path in his painting development. After some experimentation with different techniques he began to paint in mosaic style. Hugo and I tried to convince him that mosaic was a different art form, tied to the natural limitations of stone, but it was to no avail. His eyes deteriorated rapidly because of the painstaking work of painting each tiny mosaic separately. His half-dozen mosaic paintings were unique, but afterwards he was only able to adjust and correct existing paintings. He couldn't make new ones anymore due to poor eyesight.

It was fascinating to see how he could suddenly stop in front of a picture that he had finished ten years earlier and find something wrong. Within seconds he would place the old painting on his easel and start mixing oil paints for the long overdue correction. Once he had stopped making new paintings he had more time to enjoy his fourth-floor view of the *uiterwaard* and orchards from his fourth-floor apartment. On sunny days he could spend hours on his balcony, wearing a white cap and drinking from a large pot of tea. He remained a dedicated smoker of Van Nelle heavy tobacco.

Dad almost never left his home. Bruinier Grocery delivered his groceries and the neighbors or his sister Tiny did the laundry. Dad could be charming in coaxing people to do things for him. I found this trait unsettling. He had developed it into a fine art after years of dependency. The only time he left his apartment was to pick up his mail in the building lobby.

He blamed his odd behavior -- not being able to leave the house -- on phobias. Dad said that he felt tremendous fear about being outside and encountering unknown people. He made sure to impress people with the severity of his ailments. It made it easier for him to get other people to do things for him. When I was little, I believed that he really had problems, and I felt bad for him. But as I became older, I began to doubt some of his phobias. There were too many. Dad seemed to be looking for a comfortable way to stay at home and avoid running into situations he could not control.

Every year, Dad and I would visit his youngest sister Toos for Easter and Christmas. Before I had a car, the fifty-minute train and bus ride to Toos' home near Amsterdam was a major event. He traveled only first class because he'd see fewer people. For hours, he would nervously pace back and forth at home before leaving. He rolled tobacco for thirty cigarettes in advance to make sure he did not have to worry about running out of cigarettes. After we were on our way he relaxed and seemed to enjoy the traveling more than he would admit. He also liked the holiday celebrations themselves, especially the Dutch gin. He drank much more than his customary one or two gins. Within minutes of returning home after each trip he moved back into his role of the phobic person who could hardly leave his house to pick up the mail. He did not want to enjoy life too much. It was too risky.

Dad and his only brother Louis lived two miles apart. They were not close personally and Dad never visited his brother.
Occasionally, Uncle Louis would stop by to see Dad. A visitor had to pass by my dad's kitchen window before they could ring

his doorbell. If he was drinking gin and saw the profile of his brother in the kitchen window he'd say: "Oh God, it's Louis."
He'd get up quickly to hide the glass and gin bottle before opening the door.
"Hi, Louis, would you like some tea?"
Dad's gin was precious to him. I didn't think that my uncle drank gin but Dad did not want to take the risk.

My uncle never stayed for long: he just wanted to say a quick hello. He found it hard to talk to his brother about current events in Tiel because Dad usually did not know what was happening.

One afternoon, Uncle Louis appeared unexpectedly. He was drinking tea with me because Dad was busy in another room fixing a lamp.
"August, did I ever tell you about the nurse in the Culemborg hospital I spoke with on the day your Mom died?" Uncle Louis asked.
"No. I never heard about it," I said.
"I was looking for you, August, because I needed to take you with us to the hospital in Utrecht. I asked at the hospital reception and one of the nurses said that you were with the priest in his office. She said she would take me to the priest's office. It was on the other side of the hospital, in the lower level area.

On the way to the office, she told me:
'My shift had just started. I was tired because I had gone to the movies with friends yesterday and we had stayed out late. When they wheeled her in, I was awake right away. Some kind of acid, it happened about thirty minutes ago, the paramedic said. I tried to calm the lady but it was hard because she was moving around wildly. She was having trouble breathing. I asked Jeanette, my assistant, to get Father Dave. I knew he always came to the hospital right after early Sunday morning Mass. Doctor Versteeg was on ER duty that morning. He told me to call Utrecht to prepare for an emergency. He also asked me to alert the ambulance people downstairs.
The lady's husband, who looked very sad, wore a dark green raincoat. Father Dave arrived quickly and administered the Last Rites. He seemed shaken himself. Jeanette had come back and tried to restrain the lady as she moved back and forth ever more violently. Jeanette was exhausted afterwards. In the middle of the Last Rites two children came in. You could tell that the older one was a son. He looked like his father as he stood next

to him to pray. The other child, who is now with the priest, took a few steps into the ER. He stood there looking at his mother for a while. Then he turned around and left the ER. He seemed in shock and I followed him. He had put his head on a table outside. When I put my hand on his shoulder he started to cry. I tried to console him but he kept his head on the table. He never looked up.'

Dad had finished his repairs and had joined us at the table. He was moving around uncomfortably as Uncle Louis ended the story.

"Want some more tea, Louis?" Dad said after a while.

"No, Charles. I think it's time to go."

Uncle Louis got up and picked up his coat from the chair.

"See you later."

Before I could say much in return, he was out the door. Dad was following him closely as he walked past our kitchen window. Dad wanted to make sure he didn't return unexpectedly and catch Dad with a full bottle of Dutch gin.

"That was quite a story, Dad, wasn't it?" I said.

"Louis always likes to talk," Dad responded.

Silently, he picked up his brother's cup and rinsed it meticulously under the kitchen tap.

In my second year of college I noticed that Dad was not entirely without company. He had gotten to know two women who were members of a local 'phobia' group. Somehow, Dad overcame his reclusive mindset and got in touch with the group. He probably didn't go to any group meetings but soon after the initial contact, two well-dressed, attractive women in their mid-fifties visited his apartment. Their names were Johanna and Christa. Both were married. Initially they came together but after several months they started visiting on their own. Johanna and Christa seemed to overcome their phobias when they visited Dad and I strongly believed they were not limiting their discussions to phobias.

I was home one day when Christa was visiting. Dad was charming and nice. He could change completely in the presence of a good-looking woman. Maybe that's why he always sounded relaxed when he talked to me about my future girlfriend.

"Christa, please meet my son August. He is home from college for a few days."

Dad raced to get tea ready. For the occasion he had purchased very expensive cookies. I had never before seen them in our house.
"Christa, do you want something with your tea," he said with a smile.
"Yes, please, Charles."
It had been a long time since I heard somebody say 'Charles' that way.
I noticed he had fresh cut flowers on the table. That was also new. I wondered who had gotten them for him.
I talked a bit about college, and made myself unavailable within five minutes, leaving the house for an errand. Dad just wanted to show me to Christa. There was no need for me to stay any longer.

Johanna and Christa visited Dad frequently. He also told me that he had been visiting them at their homes. Their husbands were probably absent at the time. He was getting really close to Johanna and she didn't seem to mind the attention. He had started to paint a portrait of her. I was reminded of the large painting he had made when he was young to impress the pretty girl in the store. The girl never saw the painting after Dad found out she was engaged to a motor cycle driver. It had been stored for decades in humid attics when Dad found out that it had become moldy. To save the painting he had to cut it up in smaller pieces. The largest remaining piece was still a dominating presence in Dad's living room.

After two years, Johanna and Christa's visits ended abruptly. Dad said little about it but I believed that the husbands had objected to the frequent encounters. He was probably glad that neither husband ever visited him.

When I visited Dad from college, I continued to look for opportunities to find out more about what happened with Mom. The best chance was at night when Dad relaxed a bit. He loved to drink his daily *bokmaatje* gin. It was seventy-six proof and it came in a clear, square bottle with a tidy white label. Relishing the thought of drinking his *bokmaatje* at the end of the evening, he would settle down in his chair, holding his metal tobacco box, and would listen to records of Schubert, Chopin or Beethoven. He was very frugal about drinking from his own gin bottle and had only one drink each night. Unless it was a special occasion, when he had two. I couldn't recall many special cases. At the occasional wedding or when he visited his sister Toos he lost his frugality. After all, it was other people's gin.

If he seemed in a good mood, I would raise the topic of Mom. Early in the evening, he talked about how nice and beautiful Mom was and 'that she is in heaven now with the angels.' But I wanted to hear more. As he sensed that I was trying to probe deeper, he tensed up and the smile disappeared from his face.

"Wasn't there anything else the doctors could have done, Dad?"
"They tried everything, August. Librium, Valium, sleeping pills, headache medication, so much I could not keep track of it. We had a medicine cabinet full of the stuff. Your mother could not sleep anymore toward the end. She'd keep Hugo, you and me awake. That's when the doctor decided she needed rest in a special place, in Vught. The doctor said that if she could stay there for several months it could help to turn things around."
"Why did she not get better?"
"Oh, August, how can I know if even the doctors could not find the reason?"
He was becoming irritated and the discussion was growing tense.
"Oma told me that Mom had to work too hard in the business and that's why she got sick."
"Oh, that Brouwers family! They have no clue what really happened. Your Mom had not been doing much business work for several years before the real problems started. She told me she never got much support from her family and late one night, a few months before she died, she told me she felt sorry about the problems she had caused. She was ill, August. Something was not right with her and the doctors weren't able to do much about it."
"Are Hugo and I going to have the same problems?" I asked.
"Oh, August, don't worry. You're fine. There is nothing wrong with you."

His words did not reassure me. He tried hard to sound convincing but too much doubt lingered in the background. Of course, he had said himself that he did not know what happened to Mom, not even the doctors did. So how could he be so sure that Hugo and I would be fine?

He never looked at me when he spoke about these things. At the end of the discussion he was silent, the edges of his mouth turned down in a melancholic expression. I didn't know what to say next. Dad would get into this quiet, sad state that automatically cut off any further conversation. Usually, I got up and went into my room for the rest of the night. That would be the end of our talk.

Dad was deeply embarrassed by his wife's mental illness and suicide. His shame was aggravated by Mom's family who firmly believed he had not been a good husband and had pushed my mother over the brink. In their mind, Dad was a slave driver who expected his wife to both take care of two young children and assist him in the business.
My mom's family also troubled by Dad's reclusive, phobic behavior. They knew Mom missed going out in public. She was a good dancer and a superb swimmer. Not only was Dad neither a swimmer nor a dancer but he did not even try to do any activities like that. He always stayed at home without any apparent urge to go out.

Dad and I never fully discussed what happened to Mom. Dad always put up a wall, as if he resented conversation that was personal. To him 'personal' and 'vulnerable' were similar. Both were to be avoided. Suddenly, he would say that I needed to respect his privacy. 'Privacy' was one of the very few words he pronounced almost perfectly in English. I kept looking forward to that revealing moment, but in twenty years it never came.

21

A Goodbye

In the early 1980's, I moved to Chicago to attend graduate school. Dad was now the only one left in The Netherlands because Hugo had taken a job with an oil company and worked abroad. I expected that Dad would urge me to stay in Holland but instead he encouraged me to go to the U.S. He had always held great hopes for the education of his sons. Also, he admired the United States. Because he had grown up during the Depression and World War II, the U.S. was to him the country of his heroes, Franklin Roosevelt and Harry Truman.

At the end of the summer, I visited Dad a last time before leaving. "Holland is so small. I like it that you are going to a country where you will have space," he said.

It sounded strange for a man who had always preferred the smallest spaces for himself.

"Do you want some more tea, August?"

He carefully poured the tea and put a little bit of milk in it – to kill the caffeine, he said. He had a well-worn teapot cozy to keep the teapot warm.

I would miss drinking tea with him.

When I told him I needed to leave he said he would accompany me to the bus station. He had never done that. Sometimes he would go down to the lobby, waving to me behind the outside door. But this time was special.

We waited for five minutes at the station. Several strangers silently joined us. Interestingly, Dad wasn't nervous. He even started a conversation with a person next to him. It always struck me that his phobias seemed to disappear once he was actually outside of his house.
I took a seat at the back of the bus and waved to Dad until he had become a small dot in the distance. I was on my way to America.

I called Dad at least every week from Chicago to find out how things were going. His eyesight was getting worse and he was having trouble with high blood pressure. Otherwise, he seemed happy with his life. Despite his outdoor phobia he had taken up biking and regularly went out for small trips in the area. He closely followed German TV. He hated Dutch TV programs.

I met Julie toward the end of my first year in the U.S. and we started to date. She would be leaving Chicago in the next few months to go to a law school out East. It looked like we would be separated soon. A week after our first date she was accepted at the University of Chicago Law School. She stayed in Chicago and we continued to see each other. We became engaged on Christmas Day in 1983 and got married in June of 1985.

Five months before our wedding Dad suffered a severe stroke. A few weeks earlier, he had fallen off his bike and couldn't remember what caused him to fall. I spoke with him by phone the day after the stroke. His speech had been affected and he had a great deal of difficulty walking. After I finished talking with him, I cried. It was the first time I realized that he might die soon. With therapy, Dad's speech improved but he was barely able to move around his apartment anymore. Over the next year, his health gradually declined.

When I visited in the spring of 1986, I noticed that his hands felt cold and lifeless. He needed to stay in the hospital for one week. In the summer of 1986, we looked at senior citizen centers in the area His own place meant everything to him but he knew that it was time to consider alternatives. After visiting four local centers, I completed the application forms for the one he liked best. Because one piece of information was missing I asked him to mail the form himself. I felt relief that he had agreed to move into a senior citizen home.

On my last day in The Netherlands, Dad and I visited the forests near Nijmegen and he enjoyed the trip very much. When we said goodbye he smiled and thanked me for all the things I had done for him.

One week later, I called and asked him about the forms for the senior citizen home.

"Oh August, you know, I have thought about it and I decided that I should wait a while before I move into a senior citizen center."

"But you agreed to do it when I visited you," I said, stupefied.

"Well, I have had some time to think about it and I believe it's better this way."

I knew I could not persuade him, certainly not over the phone.

"Whatever you feel most comfortable with," I finally said, resigned to leave it alone.

He had made up his mind to stay at his own place.

Three months later Dad died. After hearing the news, I sat in a chair for several minutes, slowly realizing that I would not be able to say goodbye to him. I called Dad's doctor, who spoke in matter-of-fact tones about Dad's bleeding stomach ulcer and how he had died in his sleep. I asked the doctor what his last minutes must have been like.

"He died in his sleep without pain," the doctor said.

After the call I played a record of Chopin's nocturnes. Dad and I often listened to music together. The nocturnes sounded beautiful. I cried.

When would we talk again?

Julie and I left from New York for the funeral several hours after we heard the news. It was still dark and raining when we arrived at Amsterdam. We traveled by car to Tiel. I was surprised by my desire to see Dad. The funeral director warned me that the bleeding had not totally stopped yet but I told him I didn't mind. Dad looked peaceful. A tiny bit of blood had oozed out from the sides of his mouth. The funeral director assured me that it would be taken care of before the funeral.

Next, Julie and I visited the neighbors who had kept a watchful eye on Dad. They noticed that he hadn't been drinking his tea that morning.

"I'd always see his bald head just above the top of his chair."
He paused.
"I took the key to get in and I found him in the bedroom. My wife had to throw out the sheets. I hope she gave the right clothes to the funeral director."
"Yes, thank you, you picked the perfect suit," I said.
"She felt horrible that she threw out his rosary with the bed sheets. He apparently always slept with his rosary."
"It's no problem."
I thanked them for their help.

It was time to go into his apartment. They had told me that new people were to move in within 10 days. The apartments were in high demand in Tiel. Just like Dad, people liked the view of the *uiterwaard* and the apple orchards.

On Thursday, I visited the *pastorie* of the St. Dominicus Church to make the final arrangements for Dad's Saturday funeral service.
Pastor Van der Koop was old. His face looked wrinkled and worn. His sole youthful feature were the keen eyes looking over his reading glasses.
"The music for the service is all set, Mr. Hendrich told me."
"That's right, Father."
"Good. You'll have two cars for the immediate family. They will follow right after the hearse."
"Yes."
"I need some information from you about the deceased so I can include it in my homily."
"Here's a brief write-up. Let me know if you need more."
"Excellent. We should be all set for Saturday."
He put the page in a white folder and carefully filed it in a desk drawer.
"Well, is there anything else we need to discuss?" the priest said.
"I heard that Father Vis is now in the Tiel parish. Is that true?"
"Yes, you're right. He transferred from Culemborg several years ago." "Would it be possible to meet him? My mother received the Last Rites from Father Vis."
"Of course, let me see if he's in."
The priest left the room. He returned two minutes later, accompanied by another priest. I got up to shake his hand.
"Good morning, Father. My name is Swanenberg."
"Father Vis. What can I do for you?"

"I wanted to meet you. Twenty years ago you were the priest at Culemborg hospital who administered the Last Rites when my mother died."

"That's a long time ago. I was in Culemborg at the time, that's right."

"My Mom swallowed hydrochloric acid and she died later that day at Utrecht Hospital. It was the day after New Year's Day 1966."

Father Vis scratched the back of his bald head.

"It's been awhile..." he said softly.

"I was the ten-year old who stayed in your office. I remember you had lunch. My uncle picked me up later."

Father Vis lifted his head. It was coming back to him.

"Let me see. You're right, it was on a Sunday after New Year's Day.

I had just arrived at the hospital after early morning Mass. I was always in my hospital office on Sunday morning."

He paused.

"This nurse, a brunette, knocked on my door and said that a very seriously ill woman in the emergency room required the Last Rites. I asked her if she knew who it was. She said she didn't know her name but she told me that the woman wasn't old, maybe just forty. It wasn't a car accident, because she did not see any blood.

I remember, I was puzzled. You know, I kept good tabs on my people in the parish, particularly the ones that were frail and sick, but I didn't know of anyone who was around forty. I told the nurse that I would be there right away and that I just needed to put on my robe. A minute later, I rushed into the emergency room.

I recognized your Mom's face. She usually sat with her children toward the back of the church. I had not seen her in church recently. As I got my prayer book ready to start the Rites, one of the nurses whispered 'suicide attempt, she drank acid' in my ear. I was shocked. I had seen it before, but it was so new every time. A tear was coming down my cheek as I began to pray. Your Mom was in pain, she could hardly breathe. She must have swallowed something really bad. Her husband stood next to me, his head down. He was still wearing his raincoat.

In the middle of the Rites your Mom started to scream and I began to pray louder. At that point the door opened and two children came into the room. One teenager, around fifteen, and the other maybe nine or ten. That must have been you. The

older boy moved right next to his father. He looked poised, and folded his hands to pray with us. You stopped after a few steps, looking intently at us. In a quick motion you turned around and left the room. It almost seemed you were angry.
I finished my prayers. To my surprise your father asked his son to accompany your Mom in the ambulance. When I left the room I saw you sitting at the table, alone. Your father asked me if you could stay at the hospital until they could arrange for a car to take you to Utrecht. I told him that was fine and that I would ask a nurse to take you to my office. You were sad and withdrawn. You came to my office and you sat in the chair opposite from my desk. You did not want to eat anything and I ordered a meatball for myself. You hardly said anything and you were looking away most of the time. I could tell from your eyes that you were angry. To be honest, I felt relieved when they picked you up for the car trip to Utrecht.
After that, I called the brunette nurse for some fresh coffee and a chance to chat."

I thanked Father Vis. The memory of his old hospital office had made him smile.
"It was nice meeting you again," he said in a friendly manner.
He turned around and left the room.
He had a good memory for the color of a nurse's hair, I thought.

Dad's funeral was at St. Dominicus in Tiel, the church he rarely attended. A thick morning fog filled Tiel's streets and it was very cold. My closest friends from college had all come to the funeral and the number of people in church was larger than I expected. Dad was a loner and two nights earlier I had had a nightmare that the church would be empty. Frits Hendrich, the brother of my friend Gerard, played Bach and Haendel on the church organ. Dad loved to listen to records of church organ music and I was happy that Frits, who was the chief church organist, was playing for him.
As we left church, walking behind the priest and my dad's casket, I acknowledged my friends' presence by quickly nodding my head. The cars moved slowly to the cemetery through the dense fog. The mist had tightly wrapped the burial site, hiding the small cemetery chapel from our view. It was impossible to see the graves on the other side of the cemetery. The ceremony was short; it was too cold for long speeches. Hugo thanked the guests and invited them to the traditional Dutch wake: coffee, sherry, and gin in the local restaurant.

The small restaurant was filled to capacity. Dad's siblings were all there. It was the first time I had ever seen them together. It must have been a reunion for them, too.
I decided to sit down with Mom's sisters, Aunt Fie and Aunt Netty. They were nicely dressed, enjoying their coffee. Neither one had ever liked Dad.
"How are you doing, August?" Aunt Fie asked.
"I'm fine. It's been busy, but I'm OK."
I ordered another coffee.
Aunt Netty lit up a cigarette. She looked worried.
"You know, August, I was only ten when your mother got married," Aunt Fie said with a quiet voice.
Aunt Netty nodded her head in agreement.
"You were the baby sister," I said to Aunt Fie.
"I loved Riny's visits with the new baby. I held Hugo in my lap and cuddled him. Look at him now." She pointed to my brother who was at the other end of the room.
"We are all getting old," Aunt Netty said in a melancholy tone.
Aunt Fie was not finished.
"August, you were a toddler when I went to the sanatorium for tuberculosis. I was seventeen. That was a very hard year for me."
She looked at me, smiling faintly.
"But that was nothing compared to what Hugo and you went through," she continued.
"After I came back from the sanatorium I noticed that Oma was spending more time at Riny's house. She remained quiet about it but I sensed that something was wrong."
She paused.
Aunt Netty and I were waiting for her to continue.
"When Oma mentioned that a doctor examined your mom at home I asked her what was going on. She told me that Riny was tired and needed some rest. Riny was worried about the house because she had seen new cracks in the front wall and she wanted to move away from the Hoogeinde. She wanted to leave Tiel."
Aunt Netty raised both hands in exasperation, and said: "Of course, that house was just fine. It's been fine for twenty years. A family just moved in this year and did some work on it. It looks beautiful now. Doesn't it, Fie?"
Aunt Fie sipped her coffee, and nodded her head.

She continued: "After you moved to Culemborg, your Mom became worse. Hugo was busy helping out at home and you visited often with us, staying over for several days. We spoiled you with new toys. I took you to Ouwehands Zoo in Rhenen and to the Sound of Music at *Luxor* theater. Do you remember?"

"Yes, of course. Those were special events. I never went out otherwise," I said, slightly embarrassed.

"You were asleep at the end of the movie. I had to wake you up."

She said it lovingly.

I touched her hand as I got up.

"I'm going to say hello to Aunt Toos."

Aunt Toos was Dad's youngest sister. She had very dark hair. There was little resemblance with her older, blond-haired sister Tiny. Aunt Toos strongly preferred to look classy in public. She was tense about the proper dress and manner, often criticizing those who did not measure up in her eyes.

"Hello, Aunt Toos. How are you?" I said politely.

She was at the table with her daughter, Christine.

"Hello, August. I thought Hugo's speech a the gravesite was a bit short. Didn't you?"

She could always point to something that was wrong in any ceremony.

"It was cold. I think most people wanted to be inside," I said.

There was a brief silence.

"You and Mom went out a lot when you were young, didn't you?" I continued.

I knew she loved to talk about this.

"Riny was my best friend when I was a teenager. We loved to go out together in Tiel, dancing and frolicking," Aunt Toos said. "Your Mom liked sports and she danced very well. We loved the masked balls, spending much time on our costumes, surprising our friends with special outfits."

Aunt Toos looked much younger when she spoke about this.

"At one masked ball your Mom and I dressed up in black-and-white robes with gramophone record designs and hats that looked like records. We had made opposite-color versions of the same dress. We looked stunning on the dance floor, and Riny loved it."

"How did Dad get to know Mom?" I asked.

I had never heard how they met. I knew it wasn't on the dance floor.

Aunt Toos was surprised by my question. She moved her hand back and forth over her single-strand pearl necklace.
"Charles met Riny when she visited at my home one day shortly after the War ended. I was nineteen years old and Riny was still eighteen. Charles had just turned thirty-one. He was still living at home.
Charles at once took a liking to her. After all, she was a nice-looking, young girl. But he was shy and awkward in approaching her. I had to coach him a lot to make sure that he did it the right way. He was not outgoing, spent all of his time at home, and had not really met any girls. This was his big opportunity."
She smiled at the word 'opportunity,' still proud, forty years later, of her matchmaking.
"They dated for several years after the end of the war. In 1948, Riny went to Neuchatel, Switzerland for a one-year au pair stay with a Swiss doctor's family. She had had a Swiss boyfriend, the doctor's son. Your Dad had pleaded with her to return to Tiel. Ultimately, early in the summer of 1949, she did leave Switzerland, and took a job as an executive secretary. She started dating your Dad again and by the end of 1949 she was pregnant. Your mom and dad hastily put together a wedding. She hid her disappointment well, but the wedding was not what she wanted. She did not wear white and she had been quite sick throughout the autumn, in the first three months of the pregnancy. Riny's mother was furious with her about the unexpected pregnancy, and Riny suffered under her relentless comments. She also had to give up her job. Charles tried to be supportive, but I believe he didn't sense how much she missed her job. We did not see her or Charles often after her wedding. Once Hugo was born, she was busy in the house, helping Charles with his photo business and taking care of the new baby."
The smile on her face was gone. She looked serious.
"Shortly after you were born, my first baby was born. After that, I saw Riny only on special occasions. I noticed that she often looked haggard and tired."
She took a handkerchief out of her black leather purse and wiped her eyes.
"Christine, get me some water, please," she whispered to her daughter.
"I always expected Riny to shake off her illness. I thought of Riny as the vibrant outgoing woman who went to parties and

costumed balls and had a great time. Her life changed so much after she got married."
Her last words were barely audible and she was looking down, moving her right hand up and down the necklace.
"I am sorry," I said awkwardly.
Christine had returned and handed her the glass of water. She took two sips, holding the glass carefully in front of her.

After the funeral I started cleaning up Dad's apartment. In his bedroom I found several books with Uncle Louis' name handwritten on the inside cover. The books were still in good shape and I called my uncle to ask him about them. He was eager to get them back. Dad had borrowed them many years ago.
Uncle Louis lived close to Dad's apartment in a relatively new row house in the western part of town.
He quickly came to the door after I rang the doorbell.
"Hi, August. Come in."
"Thanks. Here are the books."
I put the stack on a nearby table.
"That's fine. Just leave them there," my uncle said.
"Would you like to have some coffee?" he asked.
"Sure."
My uncle gave me coffee and sat down. He immediately started talking.
"Charles was an odd man. Mind you, my brother was not crazy. He just acted strangely, occasionally. I remember when he was inducted in the Army. He was the oldest child at home and, so, the first one to go into service. This was in the Thirties and people took the draft seriously because Germany was becoming a threat to Holland. Charles hated going. He could not stand guns, not even as a child. And he hated fighting: I always won fights with him easily. He looked dejected when we said goodbye at the train station. He was back in three days. We never found out what had happened and we were afraid to ask. He was withdrawn, even more so than usual, for several weeks."
Uncle Louis was playing with his spoon, ticking on his cup. He wasn't done yet.
"Our father demanded something special from Charles because he was the first-born. Charles was supposed to be the leader, good at sports and excellent in school. Grandpa was very traditional and his demands made Charles tense. I think Charles felt the burden his whole life. Even when his dad was in his

eighties and had been in a nursing home for years, Charles would become nervous when he visited. Reverently, he'd be sitting on the bed opposite wrinkled old dad, saying little. Our dad did most of the talking: he was accustomed to being the center of attention. On one of our last visits to the nursing home, your Grandpa was talking about the ocean splashdown of a Gemini spaceflight that he had just watched on TV. After we left, Charles could not hide his admiration.
'The old man.... he still knows what's going on.'
Charles himself was not interested in spaceflights.
Charles believed he didn't live up to Dad's expectations. He often talked about how severe his Dad had been: he did not recall any tender moments with him."
My uncle looked tired. He took off his glasses, wiping his eyes. Still, he continued:
"Charles had little talent for business. He had an artistic and philosophical streak that our Dad did not like. When he was 15, Charles stayed in his bedroom for days writing about 'The Certainty of Knowledge.' In meticulous handwriting, without corrections, he wrote down how hard it was to know something. He was proud of his achievement because he did it without any education in philosophy.

    One time, he painted a picture that was 8 feet high and over 12 feet long. He didn't tell anybody why he was doing this but one night, after he had a few beers, he said that he was making it for a pretty girl he had once seen in our store. I asked him who it was. From his description, I recognized Jennie right away. I knew she was engaged. Your dad was devastated by this news. I told Charles that Jennie's fiancé drove a motorcycle. He did not touch the picture again as far as I know. It was something mythical, with horses galloping in the sky. I didn't understand why he was doing this for somebody he did not even know."
My uncle shook his head and looked at me. He smiled.
"Want some more coffee?"
"No thanks. I'm fine."
"You don't mind me talking like this, do you?" he asked.
"No, I'd love to hear more."
"OK. I wasn't sure."
He got some more coffee and sat down.
"I was happy for your dad when he became engaged to Riny. We had been worried about him. After all, he was over thirty and there was no girlfriend in sight. My youngest sister Toos

put him in touch with Riny. Those two girls were best friends at the time. Riny was an attractive girl. Still in her late teens when they first met. Then one day, it turns out she is pregnant.
Obviously, their wedding was a low-key affair. They first rented a floor on the Hoogeinde Street. Charles did the photo developing for my new business from his home. Later they were able to buy the house. They were busy every summer and every Christmas and Riny helped in the business as much as she could. In the summer, they sent you off to a camp or to Riny's parents so Riny could work full-time for the business. She looked tired at the end of summer. Hard to run a household and work long hours on the side. I sensed that my brother did not really appreciate all the work Riny did. In his own little way he could be a real slave driver. He gave her a little notebook and made her write down every darn penny she spent.

Her first nervous breakdown came in 1960, you must have just been about five years old. The doctors prescribed rest, rest, and more rest. But Riny's problems did not go away. She had some good stretches, often for weeks at a time even, but with every new breakdown things seemed to get worse. After two years, she was seeing a psychiatrist who gave her more medication. Charles had to run the show on his own during the summer. It was hard on him. Too much work comes in all at once from the union holidays. I asked Charles and Riny to join me on my trip to Lugano. I visited Switzerland every year in the fall. Things were quiet in the store and I could take my vacation. To my surprise, Charles did not object. I was sure he was going to raise hell about the expense but this time he did not seem to mind. I figured things were serious with Riny.
I enjoyed that vacation very much. Must have been at the end of 1964. Everybody was in good spirits and we took great pictures on our walks through the countryside. I remember Riny standing near a mountain stream, smiling. She was playful, walking quickly on the rocks next to the stream. "Come on up, lazy!" she cried.
After we returned to Holland, she went downhill quickly. Maybe it was the drudgery of daily life or the incessant fall rains after the sunshine in the Swiss mountains. Anyway, by early 1965, she was hospitalized for the first time. A few months later, back home, she tried to slash her wrists. Your dad was a basket case. I took as much work out of his hands as I could that summer, but he was still busy. Riny couldn't help him anymore. Even the household items were being neglected.

Your brother Hugo was picking up the pieces, at home as well as in the business. The boy had just turned fifteen, for Christ's sake.

In November, Riny took an overdose of sleeping pills and was in the hospital for several weeks. She had become a regular at the mental institution in Vught. I drove you there for Sunday visits several times.

Riny was growing more remote each time we saw her. She complained about her torn stockings, but she did not talk to you or Hugo. She was back at your house for Christmas and New Year, and, from Charles' accounts, the visit went spectacularly. Riny was feeling much better. Then I got Charles's call on Sunday morning, just after New Year's Day."

He stared in front of him, mechanically ticking his spoon on the cup. "Thank you," I said quietly.

I got up to leave.

It was time.

Dad kept his personal notes in a small orange photo paper box. He hid the box in the living room bookcase and carefully stacked books around it. The bookcase remained locked at all times.

I found the box when I started cleaning up Dad's living room. I hesitated to open it. Dad had been so protective of his personal life. I did not want to take advantage of his death to snoop in his papers. But I was curious and I told myself that there might be relevant things in the box.

I found some pictures of Mom that I had seen before. There also was an old group photo of Dad's trip to Montferland in the 1920's when he was an altar boy. He would mention that trip for the rest of his life.

An old piece of paper, folded over many times was at the bottom of the box. I opened the paper carefully because the folds were badly worn and the paper was starting to fall apart. Dad's handwriting was a jagged, nervous scribbling. He used abbreviations and, at first, I did not recognize the words. I put the paper on the table and continued to empty the rest of the bookcase. Half an hour later I began to decipher Dad's scribbles.

At the top of the note was an apology for not going to Confession in church. Then it said: "My ph.'s did not allow m." His phobias were the excuse for not going.

Then he listed his sins:

When he was seven he didn't warn a boy that a car was coming and the boy was hit and killed right in front of him.
He had masturbated.
He had sex before getting married.
It took a long time to read a single line of his personal hieroglyphics.
After several minutes, I stopped and carefully folded back the piece of paper. I did not want to read anymore.
I wiped away a tear, feeling sad for his lifetime of guilt.
I sat down in Dad's old chair, staring out the window at the fog.
If he felt guilty about the boy who was killed by the car sixty years ago I could not imagine the guilt he must have felt about Mom's illness and death.
I closed my eyes and fell asleep.

    Mom, Dad, Hugo, and I were in a dark cave. It was damp and chilly. An occasional bat swished past us, while we moved further into the cave. Day after day, we went ahead, shining tiny flashlights into the darkness ahead. Often, we looked back to see if Mom was keeping pace. She rested often and we stopped sometimes so she could catch her breath. Dad moved to the back if she wandered away. Twice, he kept her from falling, the second time barely catching her arm.
The cave became very dark, its paths narrowing to the width of our shoes. The occasional ray of light showed the tiny paths set against cavernous depths. We moved at a languid pace. Mom kept her head down most of the time, and we didn't talk anymore. We just moved.
Then Mom jumped, falling so deep that we couldn't hear the sound when she landed.
There was no light below and there was nothing to see.
Exhausted, we sat down on the rocks.
Dad cried, holding his head in his hands. Hugo and I stared ahead of us. I felt empty.
"I want to go now," Hugo said after several minutes.
He got up, and Dad and I followed.
We picked up the pace, swifter than before.
    I woke up, nervous from my dream, and left the apartment as quickly as I could. I wanted some coffee to really wake up.

    Later that day, I found a list of Mom's medications that Dad had kept in his bookcase. Meticulously, he had written the names of the medications and the dosages. In a separate column he had written the dates when Mom started the medication.

There were eight names on the list. Some sounded familiar -- Valium, Librium -- some names I had never heard of. I put the list in my pocket. I wanted to finish cleaning up my dad's apartment but I had become curious about the many medicines on the list. I decided to take a break and visit the library in Tiel.

At the library, I found that four prescriptions were anti-anxiety medications, while the other four were sedatives. If Mom suffered from depression, none of these would have helped: none were anti-depressants.
In fact, some of Mom's prescriptions would have been dangerous to severely depressed people. They could cause suicidal, panicky feelings and further disturb the depressed person's sleep. I recognized my mom's symptoms.
It dawned on me then that her doctors never diagnosed Mom's problems as clinical depression.
I closed the book, and looked out the windows. The branches in the oak tree were waving briskly in the November wind. I was thinking of the cave again and I couldn't help but imagine what my parents' visits to Dr. Klein, the psychiatrist, must have been like.

Dr. Klein, the specialist doctor in a white coat, would be sitting behind his large desk. Mom and Dad nervously entered the office.
"Good morning, doctor."
"Good morning."
A small pause followed.
"What can I do for you?" the doctor said routinely, in a quiet voice.
Mom described her symptoms: nervousness, anxiety, and lack of sleep. When Dad mentioned his busy summer season, the doctor interrupted him and asked how Dad's work influenced life at home. Feeling guilty, Dad would have emphasized how he tried to off-load Mom's work and allow her to have more leisure time.

The doctor would be looking very serious by now. He'd say that it was extremely important to reduce Mom's stress as much as possible, and to also relieve her of some of the household tasks. He believed that she was severely "over-stressed." Mom would have been quiet during the conversation. The doctor would have inquired about any family history of mental illness and Dad would have said that there were no problems in Mom's family. Opa's seasonal outbursts in the fall would not have been mentioned. Dad apparently did not know about them, and Mom would have been either too stressed to remember or, more likely, would have probably discounted her dad's strange fall moods. The doctor would probably not have heard anything about Dad's phobias. He would have been even more alarmed about the unusual home situation.

The doctor would have written a prescription for Valium to calm Mom's nerves, and a sedative to help her sleep. He would have reemphasized the importance of relieving Mom's stress: she must not work in the business and she needed to be relieved of almost all household responsibilities. Dad would have promised to take on the extra business work himself and to get outside help for house cleaning and laundry.

"Mr. and Mrs. Swanenberg, I'm confident this problem is temporary. With the medication and the decrease in stress around the home I expect that three months from now things will be much better. Thank you."

With a brisk motion he would hand Dad the prescription. He'd get up to shake hands with my parents.

Then he would see Mom and Dad to the door.

"Good luck," the doctor said.

"Thank you, doctor, thank you," Dad answered.

"Next, please," the doctor would say to his receptionist.

I looked around in the library. The old man was still reading his stock reports. Across the room a librarian was reshelving books. I continued my research.

I learned that in the late fifties, the first anti-depressant drugs, tricyclics and monoamine oxidase inhibitors (MAOI), were developed in the U.S. but adoption of these medications in Europe occurred later. Also, the development of Diagnostics Guides in the late 60's contributed greatly to increasingly precise diagnostics in the practice of psychiatry.

Mom had missed these medical advances by a few years. I closed the book with a loud noise. The old man looked up from his stock reports.

I was mad. It seemed that so much more could have been done.

By everybody.

That night, I had another dream. The whole family was in a beautiful white house. The lawn in the back was wide, extending far into the horizon. We all got up and walked to the back terrace, silently. Then Mom walked away from us, onto the wide lawn. She was wearing a long white dress, and she looked very pretty. Gently, the dress moved in the breeze. She turned around and looked at me. She smiled and waved. Her hair was dancing in the light wind.
    Then she turned back and continued to walk away. Dad ran after her, caught up with Mom and they began to argue. Mom quickly looked back at me several times. Then she abruptly stepped away from Dad and continued to move into the distance. She didn't look back anymore. Dad stood there, looking at Mom as she moved away.
"Dad, try again, try again. Please!" I cried as loud as I could.
He didn't hear me.
Mom became a tiny dot in the distance.
Then she was gone.

    A week after the funeral, I visited Dr. Jansen, Dad's primary physician, to thank him for his care. I had discussed Mom's death with him several times, mentioning the hectic events of January 2, 1966. Dr. Jansen shook my hand firmly and offered his condolences. He told me that an old friend from Culemborg had given him the phone number of one Dr. Van Meer. He smiled and gave me a piece of paper with a number scribbled on it.
"Dr. Van Meer is retired. This is his home number. Why don't you give him a call," he said.
"Thanks. I will."

"Van Meer speaking."
The male voice was strong.
"Hello, my name is Swanenberg. Dr. Jansen in Tiel gave me your number."
"Oh, that's right. I remember getting his call yesterday."
He seemed to know more than I did.
Dr. Van Meer continued.
 "I was the doctor who took your Mom to the hospital. I remember it well. We didn't get many cases like that."

"Do you mind telling me about it. I would appreciate it very much."

"Sure, I have a few minutes. After all, I am retired now."

"Thank you. It will mean a lot to me."

"Well, let's see. I got the call at around nine in the morning. The man was frantic. His name sounded like Swanberg or Swinburg but I did not recognize it because your Dad was not one of my patients. I was on duty that Sunday and I was a bit annoyed to get a call so early in the morning. It was immediately clear to me that this was an emergency. Your Mom had gone into the basement and suddenly grabbed a bottle of hydrochloric acid. She had taken two gulps before your Dad could take the bottle away from her. I told him to have her drink as much milk as possible. He was shouting my instructions to his son. I asked him for his address. Because it was close by I decided to take my own car. I could get there faster than an ambulance.

I ran to my car and drove away. Time was of the essence. If your mom had taken as much as your Dad had indicated, her condition was very serious. The acid would start to burn tissue soon. I wondered how much we could do at our hospital. Maybe we should move her directly to Utrecht. When I arrived, your Mom was sitting in a chair, holding a glass of milk. I remembered her wavy, dark hair. She did not say a word. Your dad handed me a green bottle with paint stains on it. He said he used the acid for his photography business. Your mom was quietly drinking glasses of milk handed to her by your brother. I told your parents to go with me to the hospital at once. Your mom was still able to walk and got into the car on her own. Her husband took a seat next to her in the back. He kept saying 'Oh Riny, Oh Riny!' I heard him mumble several times 'I should have gotten to the bottle faster.' "

"I remember looking out the window and thinking that you were an uncle who was picking up my parents," I said.

The doctor continued.

"I drove to the hospital as fast as I could. When we arrived at the hospital your Mom already had much difficulty getting out of the car and had started to convulse. She was gasping for air. We put her on a stretcher. I still remember her strangely determined gaze as an orderly wheeled her to the emergency room. No panic. I found her gaze unsettling.

I shook hands with your Dad in the corridor. 'They are going to do their best to help her,' I told him.

He looked grave but thanked me politely. Then he walked into the emergency room.
I drove back home. There was nothing more I could do.
The next day I heard your mother had died after being taken to Utrecht Hospital."
His story was finished.
After a few seconds of silence, I found the words "Thank you. I am very grateful for your story."
"You are welcome. I hope you have a good trip back to the United States. Goodbye."

The next morning I continued to clean up Dad's apartment. I found a letter written by Dad to himself, hidden in the bedroom closet. He had written it one year after Mom died. There were few corrections and the paper was hardly folded. It didn't seem that he had read it often, unlike his hieroglyphics text, hidden in the bookcase.
'I find it hard to talk about personal things. I can't understand how some people can go on and on about themselves. As if their lives depended on it. They just sit and chat. It makes me tired. I don't mind sitting alone with my Dutch gin, listening to music. It's so peaceful.
I have been in the photography business for close to thirty years. I have lost count of the black-and-white rolls I have developed in the dark room. The summer is the worst time. It's busy, just crazy with all these vacations happening at the same time. My wife helped me in the business but after a few years I couldn't count on her anymore. She was not well. My oldest son had become a great help. I would not know what I would have done without him.
As I told you, my wife had not been feeling well. Something was wrong in her head. The psychiatrist told me that Riny became stressed easily and he prescribed various pills. At first, Riny took them diligently but after a few months she didn't seem to care anymore.
"What does it matter?" she would ask. I had to work hard every day to make sure she'd take her prescribed medicine. She didn't have any hope left.
While Riny was ill, I read several books about mental diseases. I don't believe that doctors can do much about it. I only saw Riny get worse after treatment.
Last summer, she got hold of one of my shaving blades. I had carefully hidden them from her but she managed to find a used

one and cut her wrists. I found her in the bathroom just in time to stop the bleeding with towels. I screamed "Stop it! Stop it!" as I held her arms in the bathtub. She was frightened by what she had done and she did not resist my attempts to stop the bleeding. I was still trembling hours later. It had happened so quickly.

In the fall, she took an overdose of sleeping pills. Just like that. No warning. I just could not wake her up. In the hospital they pumped her stomach. Later, the doctor told me that Riny would not have survived had I found her even one hour later.

Sometimes I looked at her and I could tell she was far away. Nothing interested her anymore, not even the kids. I tried to tell her how important it was to take the medication but I knew that if I didn't pay attention she wouldn't take them.

Riny's parents didn't help much. They did not seem to understand what she was going through. Occasionally, her mother visited to help out with household chores. One night, Riny told me that she found her mother distant and cold and her father uninvolved. I couldn't tell if her comments were caused by hopelessness, or by the fact they didn't help us very much.

Riny's sisters, Netty and Fie, almost never visited. They probably stayed away from the house because I couldn't stand them.

During the months Riny lived at the institution in Vught, my brother Louis would sometimes drive us to visit her on a Sunday afternoon. Gradually, our visits to Vught became shorter. Riny did not talk much anymore and she did not answer our questions. The later visits took place mostly because we wanted to show her that we were there for her. The kids never said much on the way back. There was little to talk about. They must have felt sad visiting her like this.

Riny did well during last year's holiday home visit, and I looked forward to having her with us for a longer stay on her next visit. She was scheduled to return to Vught on Sunday afternoon, the day after New Year.

That Sunday morning, Riny and I rose early. She had slept well and looked good. I was surprised because she had told me the previous night that she didn't want to go back to Vught. At breakfast, she ate some sandwiches and afterwards she went to the kitchen to wash her dishes. Hugo and August were not up yet, the house was quiet and I joined Riny in the

A Goodbye 131

kitchen to make some tea. I noticed that she was looking around for something.
"Riny, what do you need?" I asked.
"O, nothing, really nothing," she whispered, and she left the kitchen.
I heard the cellar door open and I listened to her slippers shuffling on the cement staircase. I wondered why she was going down there.
I made my way to the cellar door, and I could hear her move a bottle on one of the wooden shelves. As I opened the door I saw her quickly open the green bottle of hydrochloric acid and take two big gulps from it. Grabbing the bottle, I stopped her from drinking more. I screamed for Hugo to get up and help me. He came running down the stairs quickly.
"Keep an eye on Mom. I need to call the doctor right away!"
Riny was silent. I told her to sit down in a chair.
Over the phone, the doctor told me to give Riny lots of milk.
Riny still appeared to be fine when the doctor arrived to take us to the hospital. He took the green bottle, still half filled.

During the ride to the hospital Riny started to be in great pain and by the time we arrived she had a lot of trouble breathing. In the hospital, someone called a priest and I started to lose hope when the priest began to recite the Last Rites. The doctor told me that they needed to take Riny by ambulance to the hospital in Utrecht. I asked Hugo to stay with her. I felt too nervous to do it. Hugo looked so poised; I was proud of him.

I called my brother Louis to pick August and me up for the trip to Utrecht. Riny died at 1:10 p.m., less than two hours after she arrived at Utrecht. She had many tubes in her mouth and it was hard to recognize her.
August had been waiting outside the hospital, in Louis' car. I couldn't break the news to him. I just told him it was serious, very serious.

When the two of us arrived home, I closed the curtains and sat down at the table in front of Riny's painting. I cried, cried, and cried. August sat opposite from me at the table. He looked around the room and didn't say a word. He looked grim.'

I put the letter down, with the memories of that day very clear in my mind. I didn't understand why I looked grim to Dad. I just remembered feeling totally lost that afternoon. Dad was crying, looking at Mom's painting all the time. But he never told me that Mom had died. I wondered if Dad felt guilty not telling me about Mom's death. He must have been afraid to tell me. Afraid he couldn't deal with my reaction.

He probably justified not telling me as a way to protect me. But it was probably protection for himself that he wanted. He didn't want to have to deal with a ten-year old screaming and crying that day, and maybe he told himself that he'd tell me later. But he didn't. Not the next day or the next week. I couldn't find a good reason for it. Dad simply nurtured his weaknesses too much. I realized that we were not really close if he could not tell me about mom's death.

He built his own prison and did not want to let anybody in. He was still in the attic of his old home on Water Street. The attic he loved so much because he would be left alone. No father to bug him with demands or errands, and no brother Louis challenging him to a fist fight. The attic where he experienced his personal freedom, prompting his philosophical reasoning at fifteen years old. Of course, he never left the attic. It became the dark room later in life. And after the dark room was gone he built himself a new kind of prison. The one where he didn't share with others so they couldn't surprise him with questions he didn't want to answer or emotions he couldn't deal with.

This way he didn't feel the guilt as much. Or so he thought. Maybe he heaped guilt on top of guilt, thickening the walls of the new prison, putting ever larger bars in its small windows. It gradually became impossible to listen to the questions from his youngest son.
Wasn't it bad enough that he was imprisoned? Shouldn't they pity him?
Of course, people pitied him less as the years went by. Everyone knew he himself held the hammer. Two or three whacks at the wall and he could be free. But he was busy burying the hammer. He wanted to be safe on his own terms, in his own prison. I still could get mad at him. He never offered his hand in help and he should have had the courage.
Instead he decided to act as a child himself.

22

One Last Sign

The cleaning out of Dad's apartment was slowly coming to an end. Most of his furniture went to the Salvation Army. None of the neighbors wanted the large breakfront that Mom had cried about so much. It now looked old-fashioned. It barely fit in the Salvation Army truck.
On Friday afternoon, I removed the last items from Dad's apartment. His little phone table, some chairs, and a few boxes. Only the dark green carpet in the living room was left. Exhausted, I rested on the carpet, and looked up at the ceiling with its intricate pattern of half-circle cement strokes.
      As I closed my eyes, I started to think about Dad's note about Mom.
Why did he write it down instead of telling me? Why was he afraid to tell me but not afraid to write it down?
For years, I had spent a lot of time thinking about Mom. She died because she wanted to, but I didn't know why. Didn't the doctors say they didn't know? Didn't my dad say he didn't know? Did I do everything to help her? Did she really love me? Did she?

      I believe the doctors made the wrong diagnosis with Mom. She had been clinically depressed, possibly with a link to her father's seasonal moodiness. Her doctor used the standard, middle-of-the-road judgment customary for Holland in their time. Most likely, he was unaware of the newest American medications. He knew, and trusted, his own methods, he said to himself. He may have been well-trained to listen to patients but may have been unaware of the hidden pieces of the puzzle in Mom's case. And I imagined my dad, failing to look for the clue he may have found in Mom's family. He could have talked to his in-laws about Opa's fall moods. But he couldn't stand the Brouwers family, and so he never asked, and consequently never found out.

As I sat in Dad's now empty apartment, I felt intense anger.
Shouldn't it have been obvious that somehow Mom's treatment wasn't working. Mom wasn't getting better but the doctors simply prescribed more of the same kinds of medication, and more of the Vught institutional lock-up treatment. All of which made things spin out of control.
I imagined a doctor receiving the news of Mom's suicide attempt and quickly issuing an order to institutionalize her. Make her go away for a while and see what happens. This is how we do it. I have handled cases like this before, he might have thought.
Mom's stay in Vught was the immediate reason for her final suicide attempt. She knew that she was going to be made to stay at Vught for a long time. I believe that Mom's relatively good mood around the holidays signaled that she had made up her mind to not return to Vught. She was permanently lost in the forced ostracism from home, her children, and her life. She was determined to end her suffering.
I don't blame her anymore.
Because of society's taboo against suicide, our family never talked about Mom's death, not even with each other. Outsiders were silent too, keeping their distance from my dad, my brother, and me. Dad kept social workers away from our house, fearful they would find him to be an inadequate parent. You didn't talk about suicide. It was embarrassing and shameful for the survivors.
It didn't matter if the survivors were kids or adults. Just pretend it didn't happen and go on with life.

So you told people your Mom was dead, killed in a car accident, instantly, suddenly. Over the years, you could even picture the bend in the road where it had happened. She was the only one in the car; it had rained that January morning, and the roads were slick and dangerous. Present the story in a dramatic,

definitive way so people didn't feel they needed to ask any questions. After several years you became really good at it.
"Was your Mom killed in a car accident? It's terrible to lose her that way," an acquaintance might say.
But you couldn't tell him she was a suicide. It didn't work.
"Your Mom committed suicide? Oh." A silence would follow with the person desperately trying to find an appropriate remark. Sometimes there was just silence, sometimes they'd say: "That must have been awful."
"Yes, it was."
And meanwhile they were thinking "People shouldn't die that way. It's the wrong way."
Usually people moved quickly away from you, finding relief in a different conversation.

So I learned about people's taboos, my own included. About the urge people have to keep demons away. Suicide was a demon. Don't talk about it. Avoid people who had the demon. Protect yourself. That boy was leprous with suicide. Stay away from him.
The rituals of taboo against suicide reinforced society's strong inherent fear of mental illness and death. The people in society who felt threatened did not hesitate to ostracize the family of a person who completed suicide.
Of course, I am not a leper.
But I didn't know this in 1966.

Dusk is settling in and, without lights, the main room in Dad's apartment is getting dark. The sun's late orange glow is reflected on the circular forms of the white ceiling. My Dad called this sort of twilight 'dusking.'
It's peaceful. I get up, slowly.
Tomorrow we'll take the carpet out.

The workers arrived at eight sharp, ready to start immediately. They were in a hurry because they needed to lay the new carpet that same day. The new residents would move into Dad's apartment in two days.

Within minutes they had pulled the old carpet from the floor, and piled the rolled-up fabric in a corner of the room. On the concrete floor, dark gray dust had formed circles around the spots where Dad's coffee table and dining table had stood for so many years. Through the dusty impressions, I could recognize Dad's path between the kitchen and the dining room. An extra pile of dust sat on the floor in the spot previously occupied by Dad's easy chair. The same chair where Dad had rolled so many cigarettes and drank his tea. A last sign, the dust had formed the footprints of his life at home.

We all paused momentarily, surprised by the clarity of the dust patterns on the floor. Quietly, we looked at my dad's floor until a passing truck broke the silence. Then, one of the workmen turned on his vacuum.

23

The Old Home

I have turned in the keys to Dad's apartment. Tomorrow I will fly back home, to the States. The fog from the last two days has lifted in Tiel. Instead, a fine rain is coming down intermittently. Occasionally, the sun is out among many dark gray clouds stretching to the horizon. I decide to drive to Plantsoen Park. When I get out of the car I accidentally step into a large puddle and my socks get soaking wet.
The white and brown pebbles on the paths of Plantsoen Park make a crisp sound as I walk around. The letters on the Gymnasium building's gable have not changed from 30 years earlier. The building is in poor shape. Loose bricks and slivers of paint are everywhere. It's in use, though, with many bikes in front. I wonder what the old classrooms look like.

Lange Street is now a one-way street, no longer dangerous to children the way it was when I was little.
I walk down the street toward the city canal. The butcher's store is still at the corner. The graffiti on its walls is very old, when Moluccans tried to hijack a train more than ten years ago. The pungent smell of meat is the same. The store has no customers. Most people are now buying their meat at Albert Heijn, the large chain supermarket at the edge of town.
City government finally demolished the old houses on the other side of the canal. My parents had discussed these houses thirty-five years ago. A long line of newly constructed light brown

houses with tidy front yards stretches to the end of the canal toward the river. The tiny houses contrast strangely with St. Maarten's church which overlooks the canal on the other side. The tower was repaired in the 1960's but not to its original height. There wasn't enough money. Dad always referred to the 'old' St. Maarten's as if the new one hardly deserved a mention.

The densely wooded area next to the church is gone. Another clean row of new houses has gone up, surrounding the church. The Bleach Field has become a large parking lot, totally filled with cars. The only time the Bleach Field is not a parking lot is when the Fair plays there each year.
The big gas tanks near the dike are gone, but the café at the Waal dike is still there. At ten in the morning, the large number of bikes in front shows that early business is still good.
A multitude of long, flat Rhine boats ply the wide waters of the Waal at Tiel. But their engines are quieter now and I have to listen carefully to hear them. I see no *parlevink* boats. The art of selling merchandise by riverboat has ended.
The large car ferry is gone, replaced by a tiny foot ferry to Wamel. Cars use the Willem Alexander bridge, several miles to the east of town.

The Kaai, the large grass field at the river where we played soccer, has become another parking lot. They poured concrete on most of the grass so The Kaai could be used throughout the year. The harbor hasn't changed, but the large hills of pebbles and sand are gone. Few ships stop at Tiel these days. The cut in the dike to Fish Market Square has been reconstructed and the Great Society building has been renovated. So has the Water Tower. From across the city walls the Water Tower and Great Society building overlook the river. The podium at Fish Market Square has finally lost its smell. I find myself pausing to take it in; I used to try to go past it as quickly as I could, holding my nose.

Uncle Louis' Voorstad photography store is gone. He retired several years earlier and none of his children wanted to continue the business. His old store is now part of a clothing store. It looks old-fashioned because the layout hasn't changed. A little further on, at the corner, the Campagne photo store appears to be thriving: modern signs and lots of customers. De Gruyter's grocery store has been empty for many years. The tiled Indonesian ladies on the back wall still toil in the rice fields. The owner of the building must not have had the time or money to remove them. Across the street a new Cooperative Store offers discount groceries.

Thieu, the brother of my friend Gerard, is now running the Hendrich gramophone store. He looks much like his Dad, busily putting new racks of CDs together. The Waltman Bakery is gone from the corner of Water Street and Hoogeinde. They lost their business to Albert Heijn's supermarket bakery. Perhaps Dad was right. He always claimed Waltman was too expensive.

Instead of one large movie theater, *Luxor* has become a multiplex with three smaller screens. It makes Dad's old home seem even bigger.

Our Hoogeinde house has been renovated. Not a single crack can be seen in the front.

24

The Flight Home

The 747 is packed. People are getting ready for the holidays, visiting family. I am on my way back to the U.S. It's been ten days since Dad died and I have finished all the major practical tasks after my dad's death. Dad's apartment is empty, ready for its new occupant. Hugo and I distributed the worthwhile items among family members. We settled up on Dad's financial assets. They were modest enough that their distribution didn't cause friction within our family.

I have now lost both parents, and, even as an adult, I face many new emotions. It's the trepidation of living without the trusted parental presence, which immediately told you where you came from. It's the permanent loss of cherished events: the visits, caring for the ill parent, phone chats, and drinking tea with milk. It's the realization you are on your own in a new way.

After twenty years, I feel that I finally understand what happened to Mom. It didn't ever happen by talking to Dad. Instead, it was from the scraps he left in the bookcase, the small notes and letters he wrote to himself that he told me more than he ever said while he lived.

I realize now that Mom's death was preventable. She did not have to go, as I once thought. Taboo dictated that little was said about Opa's seasonal moods, and few professionals

knew much about Seasonal Affective Disorder. The taboo kept a potentially valuable fact from Mom's psychiatrist. He might have taken Mom's problems more seriously, and might have prescribed different medication. The doctors continued to assume that Mom's problems were not caused by serious mental illness. Instead they maintained the diagnosis that she was simply overworked and needed to take her time to rest. Probably Dad's peculiar personality and his in-house business with its peak seasonal loads made this a plausible diagnosis.
No diagnosis could have been deadlier. It meant that Mom received inappropriate medication, compounding her problems.

Toward the end of her life, as dosages became higher and higher, medication turned depressive thoughts into suicidal ones. Her ostracism from her family and the larger society while she was confined at the Vught mental institution finally broke her will to live. Too young for so much pain and loss, the hatches inside me that allowed me to feel emotions about Mom closed immediately after she died. I would have drowned in sorrow. Hugo's kind words and Opa's hand on my shoulder were the only things that broke the overwhelming loneliness. I kept the hatches closed for years, to survive.
It was finally time to open them.

As the plane banks into a late afternoon sun in the west, I look down on midtown New York City, searching for the Empire State Building. A few blocks to the east, I can see my apartment building in Murray Hill.

I am home.

EPILOGUE

Thirty years after Mom's death, I visited my first suicide survivor meeting at Catholic Charities' Loving Outreach to Suicide Survivors (L.O.S.S.) in suburban Chicago. There was no requirement to speak, and a fellow survivor-moderator, together with a professional psychologist, was present to assist the group. Some survivors had experienced suicide only three months before. For some it had been several years ago, or, in my case, several decades ago. Some survivors came every month while others came irregularly or on special dates, like birthdays or anniversaries.

I don't know exactly why I went the first time. I think I felt a desire to somehow share my experience with fellow survivors. I said little the first time but listened carefully, touched by what people told me. Often, their experiences were similar to mine.

I remember a woman who was about thirty years old. She had lost a brother to suicide. She was very quiet. When a person remarked that her husband's suicide had come totally unexpected, several members of group commented immediately that they had had the same experience: they had never seen it coming. For the first time I spoke up. My mom's suicide did not come as a surprise, I said. After several failed suicide attempts, years of medication, and many months of institutionalization, her suicide felt like an inevitable conclusion. After a pause, the quiet woman who had lost her brother began to speak. Her brother's death, several years ago, had also seemed inevitable, she said. He suffered from manic depression, and appeared to be racing toward ending his life. She began to cry. But she continued to talk about her late brother's suicide. It may have been the first time.

We cannot prevent the birds of sorrow to fly over our heads but we can prevent them from building nests in our head.

Chinese Proverb

Acknowledgements

In the early 90's, I wrote a series of small stories. They were meant as reminders of days past, before long-ago details had faded away for good. After collecting about 25 stories, I started thinking about putting them together and the idea of a book was born. Understanding my mom's death became the driving force behind the book. There is so much a 10-year old doesn't comprehend about suicide that, without proper care and help, the suicide likely remains a black and mysterious event throughout adulthood. The book became my vehicle to finally address these events as a mature person.

I would like to thank Katie Holmgren, who was my editor in an early phase of the manuscript, and my wife Julie Browning, who edited a final draft of the manuscript. Their comments were very helpful and greatly improved the text. Of course, I remain solely responsible for the final content.

I also want to thank Father Rubey for his warm words of support. Father Rubey has contributed so much as the founder and director of Catholic Charities' L.O.S.S. suicide survivor organization.

My daughters Irene and Audrey were a permanent source of delight and inspiration, mostly because the book was hardly uppermost in their minds.

Finally, I want to thank my wife Julie for her support. She never wavered in her belief that my story should be told and for that I am very grateful.

APPENDIX- 1

SUICIDE SURVIVOR ORGANIZATIONS

The following organizations provide referrals to local support groups in the United States or Canada:
- **American Association of Suicidology (AAS)** Tel. 202-237-2280.
- **American Foundation for Suicide Prevention (AFSP)** Tel. 800-273-4042.
- **Friends for Survival, Inc.** Tel. 800-646-7322.
- **Heartbeat, Inc.** Tel. 719-596-2575.
- **Local mental health community centers and crisis hotlines.**

ALABAMA
Crisis Center, Inc.
3600 8th Avenue S., Ste. 501
Birmingham, AL 35222
205-323-7782

Day-by-Day
Florence, AL
205-766-9161

Survivors of Suicide Support Group
330 W. Ft. Morgan Rd., Apt. 1-B
Gulf Shores, AL 36542

Survivors of Suicide Hospice Cares, Inc.
Hospice Family Care
2225 Drake Avenue, Ste. 8
Huntsville, AL 35805

Heart-to-Heart Care Ministries
340 King Gap Mountain Road
Piedmont, AL 36272

ALASKA
Alaska Police Chaplains' Ministries
Chaplains Office
P.O. Box 200654
Anchorage, AK 99520
907-272-3100
907-786-8900

Fairbanks Crisis Line
P.O. Box 70908
Fairbanks, AK 99707
907-451-8600
800-896-5463 Toll-free

Appendix 1: Suicide Survivor Organizations

ARIZONA
Survivor of Suicide Groups
EMPACT, Suicide Prevention Ctr
1232 E. Broadway Road, Ste. 120
Tempe, AZ 85282
602-784-1514

Survivors of Suicide
Help on Call Crisis Line
P.O. Box 43696
Tucson, AZ 85733
602-323-9373

Survivors of Suicide
P.O. Box 4201
Yuma, AZ 85366
520-783-1860

ARKANSAS
Survivors of Suicide
3925 Renee Drive
Jonesboro, AR 72404

Survivors of Suicide
Arkansas Chapter
Little Rock, AR
501-337-1930

S.O.S. Arkansas Chapter
Route 7 Box 138
Malvern, AR 72104
501-337-1930
501-686-6957

CALIFORNIA
Grief Counseling Program
Crisis Support Services of
Alameda County
P.O. Box 9102
Berkeley, CA 94709
510-889-1104

Survivors of Suicide
Burlingame, CA
415-692-6662

Grief Counseling Project
Crisis Support Services of
Alameda County
21636 Redwood Road
Castro Valley, CA 94546

Suicide Survivors Bereavement
Group
Butte County Mental Health
592 Rio Lindo
Chico, CA 95926
916-891-2832

Hope After Suicide
15111 Pipeline Avenue #245
Chino Hills, CA 91709
909-393-2563

Sharp Chula Vista Medical
Center
751 Medical Center Court
Chula Vista, CA 91911

Suicide Survivors Support Group
for Children & Teens
880 Robles Place
Corona, CA 91720

Survivors After Suicide
Suicide Prevention Center of Los
Angeles
Hirsch Comm. Mental Health Ctr.
4760 South Sepulveda Boulevard
Culver City, CA 90230
310-391-1253 (24 hours)
310-751-5324

Spring Group/ Fall Group
Suicide Prevention of Yollo
County
P.O. Box 622
Davis, CA 95617
530-756-7542

San Luis Rey Hospital
335 Saxony Road
Encinitas, CA 92024

Bereavement Counseling Center
16255 Ventura Blvd., Ste. 308
Encino, CA 91601
818-906-8832

Fresno Survivors of Suicide Loss
P.O. Box 27256
Fresno, CA 93729
559-324-4950
559-431-8994
800-822-8448

Crystal Cathedral
S.O.S./ Survivors of Suicide
12141 Lewis Street
Garden Grove, CA 92840
714-971-4032
714-539-1429

Beyond Loss: Survivors of
Suicide
Glendale Adventist Medical
Center
Chaplain's Department
1509 Wilson Terrace
Glendale, CA 91206

New Horizons
Jackson, CA
209-223-0793

Survivors of Suicide San Diego
P.O. Box 4325
La Mesa, CA 91944
619-482-0297

Suicide Support Group
Jonathan Gilbert Jacoves
Memorial Fund
University of Judaism
15600 Mulholland
Los Angeles, CA 90077
310-476-9777 x215
213-934-7958

Survivors of Suicide
Modesto, CA
209-577-0615

Suicide Prevention
Crisis Line of Volunteer Center of
Napa County
1820 Jefferson Street
Napa, CA 94559
707-252-6222

Tri City Medical Center
4002 Vista Way
Oceanside, CA 92056

L.O.S.S. (Monterey Co.) &
W.I.N.G.S. (Santa Cruz Co.)
Suicide Prevention & Crisis
Center
P.O. Box 52078
Pacific Grove, CA 93950
408-375-6966
408-642-8501

Parents Surviving Suicide
P.O. Box 1006
Placerville, CA 95667

Appendix 1: Suicide Survivor Organizations

Help, Inc.
P.O. Box 992498
Redding, CA 96099
530-225-5252

Survivors of Suicide Support Group
923 E. Gail Avenue
Redlands, CA 92374
909-792-4862
909-387-7668

Friends for Survival
P.O. Box 214463
Sacramento, CA 95821
916-392-0664
800-646-7322

Charter Hospital
11878 Avenue of Industry
San Diego, CA 92128

Clairemont Emmanuel Baptist Church
2610 Galveston Street
San Diego, CA 92110

Mercy Hospital
4077 5th Avenue
San Diego, CA 92103

Survivors of Suicide (S.O.S.)- San Diego
P.O. Box 191176
San Diego, CA 92159
619-482-0297

College Avenue Baptist Church
Teen SOS Support Group
4747 College Avenue
San Diego, CA 92115

Self Help Grief Group
Center for Elderly Suicide Prevention and Grief
Goldman Institute on Aging
3626 Geary Boulevard
San Francisco, CA 94118
415-750-5355

Survivors of Suicide Group
Santa Clara County Suicide & Crisis Service
2220 Moorpark Avenue
San Jose, CA 95128
408-885-6250
408-279-3312

Suicide Survivors Group
Hospice of San Luis Obispo County
1432 Higuera Street
San Luis Obispo, CA 93401
805-544-2266

Grief Counseling Program
Suicide Prevention & Community Counseling Services
Marin County
P.O. Box 4369
San Rafael, CA 94913
415-499-1195
415-499-1193

Suicide Survivors
Hospice Services of Santa Barbara
222 E. Canon Perdido Street
Santa Barbara, CA 93102
805-965-5555

Appendix 1: Suicide Survivor Organizations

Grief Support Services
Family Service Agency of the
Central Coast/
Suicide Prevention Service
P.O. Box 1222
Santa Cruz, CA 95061
831-459-9373

Survivors of Suicide
Santa Rosa, CA
707-542-5045

Hope After Suicide
Upland, CA
909-982-7534

Bay Area Survivors of Suicide
Vacaville, CA
707-452-8520

Institute for Suicide Prevention
1156 Morrison Street
Valley Village, CA 91601
213-386-2622

Survivors of Suicide
Contra Costa Crisis Center
P.O. Box 3364
Walnut Creek, CA 94598
800-837-1818

COLORADO
Heartbeat
West Metro-Denver
6725 Pierce Way
Arvada, CO 80003
303-424-4094

Heartbeat
3520 16th Street
Boulder, CO 80304
303-444-3496

Heartbeat
2015 Devon
Colorado Springs, CO 80909
719-596-2575
719-573-7447

Parents of Suicide
212 South Dexter Street
Denver, CO 80246
303-322-7450

Heartbeat
2956 South Wolff
Denver, CO 80236
303-934-8464

Heartbeat
1760 Spruce Drive
Erie, CO 80516
303-828-3325

Heartbeat
517 West Third Street
Florence, CO 81226
719-784-4661
719-275-7232

Suicide Resource Center of
Larimer County
7604 Colland Drive
Fort Collins, CO 80525
970-686-4126

Heartbeat
722 Centauri Drive
Grand Junction, CO 81506
970-243-2467
970-243-5162

Heartbeat
Suicide Education & Support
Services of Weld Co.
3700 Golden Street
Greeley, CO 80620
970-353-0639
970-356-1710

Heartbeat
Mission Hills Church
5859 S. University Boulevard
Littleton, CO 80121
303-794-3564
303-770-1859

Heartbeat
59215 Spring Creek
Montrose, CO 81401
970-249-2979

Heartbeat
Pueblo Suicide Prevention Center
1925 E. Orman, Ste. G-25
Pueblo, CO 81004
719-564-6642
719-544-1133

Light for Life Foundation of
America
P.O. Box 644
Westminster, CO 80030
303-429-3530

Heartbeat Teens
11252 Clarmont
Wheat Ridge, CO 80033
303-252-7553

CONNECTICUT
Survivors of Suicide
Center for Hope
590 Post Road
Darien, CT 06820
203-655-4693

Safe Place
The Samaritans of the Capital
Region
P.O. Box 12004
Hartford, CT 06112
860-232-2121

Survivors of Suicide
Middlesex Community Technical
College
100 Training Hill Road
Middletown, CT 06457
203-343-5814 for Survivors Only
203-347-4003

Survivors of Suicide
Southbury, CT
203-264-5613

Suicide Bereavement
Center for Inner Growth &
Wholeness
123B Wolcott Hill Road
Wethersfield, CT 06109
860-563-3035

Survivors of Suicide
68 Hilbrook Road
Wilton, CT 06897
203-762-7804

Appendix 1: Suicide Survivor Organizations

DELAWARE
S.O.S.
Grace United Methodist Church
Church and Morris Streets
Millsboro, DE 19966

S.O.S.
1813 N. Franklin Street
Wilmington, DE 19802
800-287-6423 in-state only
302-656-8308

WASHINGTON D.C.
Crisis HelpLine
Commission on Mental Health
Services of Washington, DC.
1905 E. Street, SE
Washington, DC 20003
202-673-9307
1-8887-WE HELP
202-561-7000

FLORIDA
Survivors of Suicide Support
Group
Altamonte Springs, FL
407-869-9617

Suicide Survivors Support Group
Boca Raton, FL
407-394-7979

Hospice of SW Florida
Bradenton, FL
941-739-8940

Survivors of Suicide
Cape Coral, FL
941-945-0338

Assure
MH Associates of Volusia County
531 South Ridgewood Avenue
P.O. Box 2554
Daytona Beach, FL 32115
904-252-5785
904-756-3198

Survivors of Suicide
First Call For Help/ Broward
County
16 Southeast 13th Street
Fort Lauderdale, FL 33316
954-467-6333
954-524-8371

Self Help Support Group
Suicide Prevention Center
3634 Shawnee Shores Drive
Jacksonville, FL 32225
904-353-2223

SOS- Lovejoy Center for
Suicidology
The Courage to Survive
825 Center Street, Ste. 35B
Jupiter, FL 33458
561-747-3165

Survivors Support Group
Lauderhill, FL
954-968-6795
954-768-0434

Suicide Survivors Support Group
Miami, FL
305-653-1023

Survivors of Suicide
Hotline & Referral/ Project Help,
Inc.
P.O. Box 7804
Naples, FL 34101
941-649-1404
800-329-7227

Survivors of Suicide Support
Group
c/o We Care Crisis Center
112 Pasadena Place
Orlando, FL 32803
407-425-5201

The Courage To Survive
Palm Beach, FL
407-747-3165

Survivors of Suicide
Mental Health Association of
West Florida
1995 N. H Street
Pensacola, FL 32501
904-438-9879
850-968-3260

Personal Enrichment Through
MHS, Inc.
11254 58th Street North
Pinellas Park, FL 34666
813-545-5636
813-791-3131

Crisis Services of Brevard
P.O. Box 561108
Rockledge, FL 32956
407-631-8944

Family Support After Suicide
Mental Health Association of
Palm Beach County
909 Fern Street
West Palm Beach, FL 33401
561-369-3800

GEORGIA
Suicide Survivors
Albany, GA
912-883-1281

S.O.S. Sandy Springs Chapter
The Link Counseling Center
348 Mount Vernon Highway, NE
Atlanta, GA 30328
404-256-9797

S.O.S. Day Group
Brookwood Center for
Psychotherapy
1708 Peachtree Street, NW, Ste.
315
Atlanta, GA 30309
404-872-8065

S.O.S. Gwinnett Chapter
4093 Menlo Way
Atlanta, GA 30340
404-256-9797
770-939-8584

Ben Hill United Methodist
Church
2099 Fairburn SW
Atlanta, GA 30331
404-505-7703

Appendix 1: Suicide Survivor Organizations

S.O.S. Support Group
Ebenezer United Methodist
Church
Stanton Road, Room 35
Conyers, GA 30207

S.O.S. Gwinnett Chapter
Summit Ridge, Room 5
250 Scenic Highway
Lawrenceville, GA 30245
404-256-9797

S.O.S. East Cobb Chapter
Lutheran Church of the
Resurrection
4814 Paper Mull Road
Marietta, GA 30067
770-998-8819

S.O.S. Marietta Chapter
56 Whitlock Avenue, Room 212
Marietta, GA 30060
770-432-1621
770-436-4090

S.O.S. Support Group
170 Daisy Place
Newnan, GA 30625
770-251-6216
770-251-6470

Healing Grief Support Group
15 Tony Nevil Road
Register, GA 30452
912-852-5117
912-764-5683

S.O.S. Riverdale Chapter
Eastside Baptist Church
70 Upper Riverdale Road
Riverdale, GA 30274
770-998-8819

Roswell Group
Rosswell United Methodist
Church
814 Mimosa Boulevard
Roswell, GA 30075
770-993-6218

S.O.S. Stone Mountain Chapter
Rock of Ages Lutheran Church
5135 Memorial Drive
Stone Mountain, GA 30083
404-939-8584
404-296-0627

HAWAII
Survivors of Suicide
Helping Hands Hawaii
680 Iwilei Road, # 430
Honolulu, HI 96817
808-521-4555

IDAHO
Survivors of Suicide
Boise, ID
208-338-1017
208-345-2350

Survivors of Suicide
1879 W. South Slope Road
Emmett, ID 83617
208-398-8231
208-345-2350

S.O.S./ Pocatello Chapter
2411 S. Woodruff
Idaho Falls, ID 83404
208-522-0033
208-524-2411

ILLINOIS
Survivors of Suicide
508 Clearwater Drive
Aurora, IL 60542
630-897-5522
630-897-9699

Survivors of Suicide
Mental Health Association of
Illinois Valley
5032 W. Burns Avenue
Bartonville, IL 61607
309-697-3342

Centralia Ray of Hope
Irvin Funeral Home
P.O. Box 1155
Centralia, IL 62801
618-532-5512

Loving Outreach to Survivors of
Suicide (L.O.S.S.)
Catholic Charities
126 North Des Plaines Street
Chicago, IL 60661
312-655-7283
312-655-7285

OPTIONS Counseling Service
3232 W. Victoria
Chicago, IL 60659
773-463-1901

Survivors of Suicide
Call for Help, Suicide & Crisis
Intervention
9400 Lebanon Road
Edgemont, IL 62203
618-397-0963

The Compassionate Friends, Inc.
P.O. Box 3696
Oak Brook, IL 60522
708-990-0010

Survivors of Suicide
Peoria, IL
309-693-5281
309-697-3342

Rock Island Ray of Hope
Office of the Coroner
1504 3rd Avenue
Rock Island, IL 61107
309-786-4451

Suicide: Survivors Gather
Fred C. Olsen Funeral Chapels
309 7th Street
Rockford, IL 61104
815-962-0782
815-399-6047

Ray of Hope
Fred C. Olsen Funeral Chapels
1001 Second Avenue
Rockford, IL 61104

The C.O.-H.E.A.R.T.S.
Behavioral Health Alternatives
337 E. Ferguson
Wood River, IL 62095
618-251-4073

Appendix 1: Suicide Survivor Organizations

INDIANA
S.O.S./ Heartbeat
2341 Winding Brook Circle
Bloomington, IN 47401
812-336-0649

S.O.S./ Heartbeat
P.O. Box 1149
Bloomington, IN 47402
812-336-9463

S.O.S./Heartbeat
16210 E. Main
Columbus, IN 47203
812-546-5820

Survivors of Suicide
Elkhart, IN
219-295-8156

Survivors of Suicide
MH Assoc. Vanderburgh County
123 N.W. 4th Street, Ste. 707
Evansville, IN 47708
812-426-2640

We the Living
4531 Highwood Drive
Fort Wayne, IN 46815
219-485-4369
219-483-4895

The Wounded Healers
921 West 45th Street
Griffith, IN 46319
219-924-5577

Community Hospital, Access Services
7150 Clearvista Drive
Indianapolis, IN 46256
317-841-5700 or 5835

Survivors of Suicide Victims
Chaplain's Office
Community Hospital Indianapolis North
Indianapolis, IN 46256
317-841-5269

Survivors of Suicide Support Group
Lafayette Crisis Center
1244 N. 15th Street
Lafayette, IN 47904
765-742-0244

Survivors
P.O. Box 1838
Marion, IN 46952
765-662-3971
765-664-9978

Survivors of Suicide
Quinco Consulting Associates
P.O. Box 550
Nashville, IN 47448

Hospice of St. Joseph County
111 Sunnybrook Court
South Bend, IN 46637
219-243-3100

IOWA
Suicide Grief Support Group
Cedar Falls, IA
319-277-5369

Suicide Survivors Group
Foundation 2, Inc.
1540 Second Avenue SE
Cedar Rapids, IA 52403
319-277-5369

Ray of Hope, Inc.
P.O. Box 2323
Iowa City, IA 52244
319-337-9890

Sioux City Broken Silence
Support Group
1801 Morningside Avenue
Sioux City, IA 51106

KANSAS
Heartbeat
217 South East Street
Oberlin, KS
913-475-3566

Suicide Prevention Program
Parsons Ray of Hope
203 Kay Lane
Parsons, KS 67357
316-421-3254

Survivors of Suicide
3019 S.E. Starlite
Topeka, KS 66605
913-267-4547
913-273-2252

KENTUCKY
Survivors of Suicide of Northern
Kentucky
48 Edwards Court
Fort Thomas, KY 41075
606-441-1958

Survivors of Suicide Support
Appalachian Region Medical Ctr.
100 Medical Center Drive
Hazard, KY 41701
800-568-2440 (KY, VA, WV)
606-277-7583

S.O.S.
Mountain Community Hospice
P.O. Box 1234
Hazard, KY 41702
606-439-2111

Survivors of Suicide
Hospice of Bluegrass
2312 Alexandra Drive
Lexington, KY 40504
606-276-5344

Survivors of Suicide
330 North Hubbard's Lane
Louisville, KY 40207
502-895-9122
502-589-4313

Survivors of Suicide
Middlesboro, KY
606-248-1678

Survivors of Suicide
Hospice Association
P.O. Box 1403
Owensboro, KY 42302
502-926-7565

LOUISIANA
Baton Rouge Crisis Intervention
Center
4837 Revere Avenue
Baton Rouge, IL 70808
504-924-1431
504-924-3900

Appendix 1: Suicide Survivor Organizations 1- 13

Survivors of Suicide
Charter Cypress Hospital
Al-ANON Room
302 Dulles Drive
Lafayette, LA 70506

Support After Suicide
3804 Gouville Drive
Monroe, LA 71201
318-323-9479
318-322-5065

Coping with suicide
406 Audubon Trace
New Orleans, LA 70121
504-865-2670
504-834-1354

Survivors of Suicide
4747 Earhart Boulevard
New Orleans, LA
504-523-COPE

MAINE
Suicide Survivors Group
Maine Medical Center
22 Bramhall Street
Portland, ME 04102
207-871-4226
207-781-4775

Survivors of Suicide
Rumford, ME
207-364-2651

MARYLAND
SEASONS: Suicide Bereavement
4706 Meise Drive
Baltimore, MD 21206
410-882-2937

SEASONS (Suicide Survivor group)
Cedar Lane Unitarian Church
Bethesda, MD 20814
301-493-8302
301-460-4677

Growing Through Grief
1535 Marlborough Court
Crofton, MD 21114
410-721-0899

Suicide Survivors Support group
Hospice Caring- Montgomery County
Gaithersburg, MD
301-869-4673

Seasons: Suicide Bereavement
13907 Vista Drive
Rockville, MD 20853
301-460-4677
301-493-8302

Griefworks- Healing from Loss
14203 Arctic Avenue
Rockville, MD 20853
301-871-3478

Suicide Survivors Group
3800 Devonshire Road
Salisbury, MD 21804

SEASONS: Suicide Bereavement
Westminster, MD
410-876-1047

MASSACHUSETTS
Safe Place/ The Samaritans of
Merrimack Valley
Andover, MA
508-688-6607

After Suicide
41 Concord Square
Boston, MA 02118
617-738-7668
617-876-4488

Safe Place
The Samaritans of Boston
500 Commonwealth Avenue
Boston, MA 02215
617-247-0220 adults
617-247-8050 teens
617-536-2460

After Suicide
Focus Counseling & Consulting, Inc.
186-1/2 Hampshire Street
Cambridge, MA 02139
617-876-4488
617-738-7668

After Suicide
850 Boylston Street, Ste. 414
Chestnut Hill, MA 02167
617-738-7668
617-876-4488

Safe Place Self-Help Support Group
Samaritans of Fall River/New Bedford
386 Stanley Street
Fall River, MA 02720
508-673-3777
508-999-7267

Safe Place/ The Samaritans of
Cape Cod
Falmouth, MA
508-875-4500

Safe Place/ Samaritans
Samaritans Suburban West
276 Union Avenue
Framingham, MA 01702
508-875-4500
508-478-7877

JANOVA Survivors Group
263 Waban Avenue
Newton, MA 02468
617-244-5249

In Memory Still
901 Main Street
Osterville, MA 02655
508-477-6771

Suicide Loss Support Group
Hospice Care in the Berkshires
369 South Street
Pittsfield, MA 01202
413-443-2994

Suicide Grief Support Group
26 Curve Street
Sherborn, MA 01770
508-653-1609

Survivors of Suicide
Forastiere Family Funeral Home
45 Locust Street
Springfield, MA 01108
413-733-5311

Survivors of Suicide
West Springfield, MA
413-734-9139

Appendix 1: Suicide Survivor Organizations

MICHIGAN
S.O.S.
Adrian, MI
517-263-7882

Survivors of Suicide
University of Michigan Hospital
1500 E. Medical Center Drive
Ann Arbor, MI 48109
313-936-4559
313-936-5800

Touched by Suicide
Samaritan Counseling Center
1850 Colfax
Benton Harbor, MI 49022
616-926-6199

Those Touched By Suicide
1775 Melton
Birmingham, MI 48009
313-646-5224

S.O.S.- North Central
527 Cobbs
Cadillac, MI 48601
616-775-3463
616-826-3865

Survivors of Suicide
Macomb County Crisis Center
46360 Gratiot Avenue
Chesterfield Twnshp, MI 48051
810-307-9100

Survivors of Suicide
NSO Emergency Telephone
Serve/ SP Center
220 Bagley, Ste. 626
Detroit, MI 48226
313-224-7000

Survivors of Suicide
Durand Library
4714 Bennington Road
Durand, MI 48420
517-743-4945

Survivors of Suicide
East Lansing, MI
517-626-6317

Catholic Social Services
202 E. Boulevard Drive, Ste. 210
Flint, MI 48503
810-235-5552

Survivors of Suicide
Flint, MI
810-232-9950

West Michigan Survey of Suicide
Grand Rapids
2548 Newberry Lane, SE
Grand Rapids, MI 49508
616-554-3265

West Michigan Survivors of
Suicide
Grand Rapids, MI
616-281-2058

West Michigan Survivors of
Suicide
West Michigan Survivors
270 Hoover Boulevard
Holland, MI 49423

Survivors of Suicide
915 Airport Road
Jackson, MI 49202
517-783-2648
734-426-0371

Appendix 1: Suicide Survivor Organizations

Gryphon Place
1104 South Westnedge
Kalamazoo, MI 49008/
616-381-4357
616-381-1510

Survivors of Suicide
Lansing, MI
517-339-1529

West Shore Survivors of Suicide
412 Ludington Avenue
Ludington, MI 49431
616-845-6854
616-845-5589

Survivors of Suicide
Marquette General Hospital
Regional Medical Center
Marquette, IN 49855

Heartbeat
404 Cherry Creek Road
Marquette, MI 49855

Survivors of suicide
c/o Hospice of Monroe
502 West Elm Avenue
Monroe, MI 48162

Survivors of Suicide
Macomb County Crisis Center,
5th Floor
Mount Clemens, MI 48043
810-948-0224

Survivors of Suicide
Risen Christ Lutheran Church
46250 Ann Arbor Road
Plymouth, MI 48170
313-677-0500

S.O.S.
Port Huron, MI
810-794-4982

Survivors of Suicide
Health Source
3340 Hospital Road
Saginaw, MI 48689
517-781-5260
517-249-4230

West Michigan Survivors of
Suicide- Muskegon
201 Dewitt Lane #101
Spring Lake, MI 49456
616-847-7827
616-766-3379

Touched by Suicide
Samaritan Counseling Center
1850 Colfax
Benton Harbor, MI 49022
616-926-6199

Survivors of Suicide
Community Mental Health
Center
701 S. Elmwood
Traverse City, MI 49684

Suicide Survivors Support group
5391 Highland Road
Waterford, MI
810-618-0040
248-673-1213
248-625-9430

Appendix 1: Suicide Survivor Organizations 1- 17

MINNESOTA
Brooklyn Park Suicide Survivors
Grief Groups
Prince of Peace Lutheran Church
7217 W. Broadway
Brooklyn Park, MN 55428

Suicide Survivors Group
St. Mary's Grief Support Center
407 East Third Street
Duluth, MN 55805
218-726-4402

West Metro Suicide Survivors
Grief Group
Oak Grove Baptist Church
5920 Golden Valley Road
Golden Valley, MN 55422
612-922-5830

Immanuel-St. Joseph' Hospital-
Mayo Health Systems
Room 4000, 7th Floor
1025 Marsh Street
Mamkato, MN 56001
507-625-4031

Men's Saturday Breakfast Group
Pearson's Edina Restaurant
3808 W. 50th Street
Minneapolis, MN 55410
952-882-1246
763-544-7315

Death Response Team
University of Minnesota
Comstock Hall- East
210 Delaware Street, SE
Minneapolis, MN 55455
612-624-4632

Suicide Survivors Grief Group
Church of Christ the Redeemer
5440 Penn Avenue South
Minneapolis, MN 55419
763-566-4063
952-944-2478

SAVE
Minneapolis, MN
612-946-7998

Survivors of Suicide
1485 White Bear Avenue
St. Paul, MN 55106
612-776-1565

Support Group for S.O.S.
Lutheran Social Service
333 Litchfield Avenue, SW
Willmar, MN 56201
320-235-5411

MISSISSIPPI
Survivors of Suicide
Jackson, MI
601-360-0814

MISSOURI
Survivors of Suicide Group
#8 Terrapin Road
Cape Giradeau, MO 63701
573-334-6508
800-780-8224

Survivors of Suicide Support
Life Crisis Services
1423 South Big Bend Boulevard
St. Louis, MO 63117
314-647-3100 or 4357

MONTANA
Surviving Friends
Missoula, MT
406-543-6132

NEBRASKA
Heartbeat
1740 Highland Drive
Hastings, NE 68901
402-463-7711

Lincoln Ray of Hope
2118 South 36th Street
Lincoln, NE 68506
402-488-3827
402-477-8610

S.O.S. Omaha
6114 Franklin Street
Omaha, NE 68104
402-558-4616

NEVADA
Suicide Prevention & Crisis Call Center
P.O. Box 8016
Reno, NV 89507
702-784-8085
800-992-5757

NEW HAMPSHIRE
Coping With A Loved One's Suicide
Derry, NH
603-329-5276

Samaritans/ Safe Place
The Samaritans of the Monadnock Region
103 Roxbury Street, Ste. 304
Keene, NH 03431
603-357-5510

Upper Valley SOS
Hospice VNH
325 Mount Support Road
Lebanon, NH 03766
603-448-5182
802-295-2064

Survivors of Suicide
Samaritans of South Central NH
2013 Elm Street
Manchester, NH 03104
603-644-2525
603-622-3836

Coping With A Loved One's Suicide
CLM Behavioral Health Systems
Salem Professional Park
44 Stiles Road
Salem, NH 03079
603-893-3548
603-434-1577

NEW JERSEY
Survivors of Suicide
P.O. Box 183
Andover, NJ 07821
973-786-5178

Survivors after Suicide CCMH
2 Park Avenue
Dumont, NJ 07628
201-385-4400

S.O.S.
Madison, NJ
201-786-5178

Survivors of Suicide
UMDNJ University Behavioral
Health Care
671 Hoes Lane
Piscataway, NJ 08854
732-235-9260

Bloomsbury Ray of Hope
419 Penwell Road
Port Murray, NJ 07865
908-835-1256

Survivors of Suicide
Community Medical Center
The Center for Kids & Family
Riverwood Building II
Toms River, NJ 08753
732-886-4475
732-505-5437

NEW MEXICO
New Mexico Grief Services
Program
Office of Medical Investigator
UNM School of Medicine
Albuquerque, NM 87131
505-272-2485
505-272-3053

Survivors of Suicide
12010 Dusty Rose Road, NE
Albuquerque, NM 87122
505-858-1240

NEW YORK
Safe Place
The Samaritans
P.O. Box 5228
Albany, NY 12205
518-459-4040
518-459-0196

Compassionate Friends/ Parents
of suicide.
Babylon, NY
516-459-0196

After Suicide/ Daisy Marquis
Jones Family Wellness Center
156 West Avenue
Brockport, NY 14420
716-637-5365
716-395-6044

Suicide Bereavement Group
Life Transition Center
3580 Harlem Road
Buffalo, NY 14215
716-836-6460

Suicide Prevention & Crisis
Service
Tompkins County
P.O. Box 312
Ithaca, NY 14851
607-272-1505

Putnam/ Northern Westchester
Resource Center
2 Mahopac Plaza
Mahopac, NY 10541
845-628-9284

A Time for Healing
c/o P.O. Box 336
Massapequa Pk., NY 11762
516-798-7881

The Samaritans of New York
Suicide Prevention Hotline
P.O. Box 1259
Madison Square Station
New York, NY 10159
212-673-3000

S.O.S- Staten Island
New York, NY
718-448-3306

Ray Of Hope- Brooklyn
New York, NY
718-738-9217

S.O.S.- Douglaston (Queens)
New York, NY
516-466-8423

S.O.S.- Flushing (Queens)
New York, NY
718-463-1639

Survivors of Loved One's Suicide
350 West 55th Street
New York, NY 10019
212-246-3117

Survivor Group
Brookhaven Memorial Hospital
105 W. Main Street
Patchogue, NY 11772
516-687-2960

Survivors of Suicide Group
1670 Old Country Road, Ste. 222
Plainview, NY 11803
516-777-1787
516-365-5810

Survivors of Suicide
Port Jefferson, NY
516-474-6061

The Compassionate Friends for Bereaved Parent
60 Atkinson Road
Rockville Center, NY 11570
516-486-3671

Nassau Long Island Survivors of Suicide
125 Minneola Avenue, Ste. 106
Roslyn Heights, NY 11577
516-488-7697
516-626-1971

Survivors After Suicide
350 Richmond Terrace
Staten Island, NY 10301
718-448-3306
718-987-9381

C.A.R.E.S./ Survivors of Suicide
New York Hospital- Westchester Division
21 Bloomindale Road
White Plains, NY 10605
914-997-5849

Surviving Suicide
2000 Maple Hill Street
Yorktown Heights, NY 10595
914-962-5593

NORTH CAROLINA
Touched by Suicide
To Life
1850 E. 5th Street, Ste. 212
Charlotte, NC 28204
704-332-5433

Triangle Hospice
Lifeline Suicide Survivor Support
1804 Martin Luther King Parkway, Ste. 112
Durham, NC 27707
914-490-8480
919-644-6869

Appendix 1: Suicide Survivor Organizations　　　1-21

Survivors of Suicide
Hickory Resource Center
328 N. Center Street
Hickory, NC 28601
704-462-1900

Survivors of Suicide
218 Wagoner Drive
Mount Airy, NC 27030

Survivors Support Group
Crisis Center of Coastal Horizons
3333 Wrightville Ave., Ste. 100
Wilmington, NC 28403

Touched by Suicide
1602-A North Lumina Avenue
Wrightsville Beach, NC 28480
910-256-3802
910-686-2812

NORTH DAKOTA
Grief After Suicide
MH Associates of North Dakota
200 West Bowen Avenue
Bismarck, ND 58504
701-255-3692
800-472-2911

Suicide Survivor Group
Hotline
P.O. Box 447
Fargo, ND 58107
701-293-6462

Friends and Family Surviving
Suicide
Northeast Human Service Center
1407 24th Avenue S.
Grand Forks, ND 58201
701-746-9411
701-775-0525

Survivors of Suicide (SOS)
Minot, ND
701-857-2230

Survivors of Suicide (SOS)
Wahpeton, ND
701-293-6462

OHIO
Survivors
Portage Path Behavioral Health
640 S. Broadway
Akron, OH 44308
330-253-9388

Survivors
Crisis Intervention Center of
Stark County
2421 13th Street, N.W.
Canton, OH 44708
216-452-6000 or 9812

Survivors After Suicide
4142 Eddystone Drive
Cincinnati, OH 45251
513-385-6110
513-729-2960

Survivors of Suicide
Cincinnati, OH
513-841-1012

Survivors of Suicide
192 S. Princeton Avenue
Columbus, OH 43223
614-279-9382

Survivors of Suicide
Suicide Prevention Center
P.O. Box 1393
Dayton, OH 45401
513-297-9096

HelpLine-Delaware/ Morrow Co.
11 North Franklin Street
Delaware, OH 43015
740-363-1835

Survivors of Suicide
Lakewood, OH
216-521-1335

Lake County Survivor Support Group
5930 Heisley Road
Mentor, OH 44060
440-354-9924
440-942-1398

HelpLine of Delaware & Morrow Co.
950 Meadow Drive
Mt. Gilead, OH 43338
419-946-1350

Survivors of Suicide
2414 Grantwood Drive
Parma, OH 44134
216-351-1137

Survivors of Suicide
P.O. Box 1407
Russels, OH 43348
937-843-6836

Survivors of Suicide
Mental Health Services- Clark County
1345 Fountain Boulevard
Springfield, OH 45504
937-399-9500

Survivors of Suicide
Toledo, OH
419-385-9205

S.O.S.
Concord Counseling Center
924 Eastwind Drive
Westerville, OH 43081
614-882-9338

Survivors of Suicide
Help Hotline Crisis Center
P.O. Box 46
Youngstown, OH 44501
330-747-5111
330-747-2696

OKLAHOMA
S.O.S.
Oklahoma City Chapter
2109 Silvertree Lane
Edmond, OK 73013
405-359-0909
405-330-8155

Survivors of Suicide
4400 W. Main, #120
Norman, OK 73072
405-447-1498
405-329-4280

Survivors of Suicide
Oklahoma City, OK
405-942-1345

Survivors
Mental Health Association
1870 S. Boulder
Tulsa, OK 74119
918-585-1213
918-663-0747

Appendix 1: Suicide Survivor Organizations

OREGON
Survivors of Suicide
Albany, OR
503-394-3707

Healing from Suicide
Medford, OR
503-772-2527

The Dougy Center (Ages 3-19)
3909 S.E. 52nd
Portland, OR 97286
503-775-5683

Suicide Bereavement Support
P.O. Box 2116
Portland, OR 97212
503-235-0476
503-699-8103

PENNSYLVANIA
Altoona Hospital Center for
Mental Health Services
620 Howard Avenue
Altoona, PA 16601
814-946-2141

Community Mental Health
Center
112 Hillvue Drive
Butler, PA 16001
724-287-0791

Survivors of Suicide
2064 Heather Road
Folcroft, PA 19032
215-545-2242

Survivors of Suicide
Fort Washington, PA
215-545-2242

Survivors of Suicide
Lancaster, PA
717-898-8239

Survivors of Suicide
200 Oxford Valley Road
Langhorne, PA 19047
215-545-2242

S.O.S.
402 Home Drive
Level Green, PA 15085
412-373-7562

Survivors of Suicide
Levittown, PA
215-545-2242

S.O.S.
3 Hospital Drive
Lewisburg, PA 17837
717-523-7509
717-524-0001

Suicide Bereavement Group
960 Century Drive
P.O. Box 2001
Mechanicsburg, PA 17055
717-795-0330

Suicides Other Victims
MH Association Beaver City
1260 N. Brodhead Road, Ste. 107
Monaca, PA 15061
724-775-4165
724-775-8523 Fax

Survivors of Suicide
37 Walnut Lane
Morrisville, PA 19067
215-736-1643
215-295-1623

Survivors of Suicide
18th & Lombard Street
Philadelphia, PA 19146
215-545-2242
215-745-8247

Western Psychiatric Institute & Clinic
3811 O'Hara Street
Pittsburgh, PA 15213
412-624-5170
412-624-2000

Survivors of Suicide
328 Park Avenue
Quakertown, PA 18951
215-536-5143
215-536-9070

Suicide Survivors Group
Catholic Social Services
33 E. Northampton Street
Wilkes-Barre, PA 18703
717-824-5766

Survivors of Suicide
100 Lancaster Avenue
Wynnewood, PA 19096

RHODE ISLAND
Safe Place/ Samaritans
The Samaritans of Rhode Island
2 Magee Street
Providence, RI 02906
401-272-4044
800-365-4044

SOUTH CAROLINA
Survivors of Suicide
P.O. Box 1981
Anderson, SC 29622
864-225-6239

Survivors of Suicide
Charleston, NC
803-744-4357

Survivors of Suicide
Columbia, NC
803-356-2874

Survivors of Suicide
Mental Health Association of Greenville Co.
301 University Ridge, Ste. 5600
Greenville, SC 29601
864-271-8888

Survivors of Suicide
223 Murray Vista Circle
Lexington, SC 29072
803-356-2874

Survivors of Suicide
Hotline
P.O. Box 71583
N. Charleston, SC 29415
843-747-3007
843-744-4357

SOUTH DAKOTA
S.O.S. Group
Heartbeat
P.O. Box 646
Huron, SD 57350
605-352-5930
605-352-6263

Survivors of Suicide
Suicide Helpline
1000 N. West Avenue, Ste. 408
Sioux Falls, SD 57104
605-336-2737
605-336-1974

Appendix 1: Suicide Survivor Organizations

TENNESSEE
Living After Suicide
Chattanooga, TN
423-875-2509

Tri-Cities Survivors of Suicide
P.O. Box 185
Erwin, TN 37650
423-735-7052
423-734-4410

The Suicide Grievers Support Group
1300 Highvue Drive
Knoxville, TN 37932
865-541-8536

Survivors of Suicide Support Groups
Crisis Intervention Center
P.O. Box 40752
Nashville, TN 37204
615-244-7444
615-269-4357

TEXAS
Suicide: The Ones Left Behind
P.O. Box 2232
Abilene, TX 79604
915-893-5015
915-893-5144

Survivors Group
Texas Panhandle Mental Health Authority
P.O. Box 3250
Amarillo, TX 79116
806-359-6699
800-692-4039

Survivors of Suicide
Hotline to Help

Austin-Travis Co. MHMR
P.O. Box 3548
Austin, TX 78764
512-703-1300
512-472-4357

Survivors After Suicide
Corpus Christi, TX 78413
512-853-1964
512-852-9665

Suicide and Crisis Center
2808 Swiss Avenue
Dallas, TX 75204
214-828-1000

Survivors of Suicide
P.O. Box 10614
Fort Worth, TX 76114
817-654-5343
817-732-6049

Crisis Intervention of Houston
P.O. Box 130866
Houston, TX 77219
713-527-9864
713-228-1505

Survivors of Suicide Support Group
P.O. Box 6477
Lubbock, TX 79493
806-765-7272
800-886-4351

Survivors of Suicide
Lufkin, TX
409-632-1514

Survivors of Suicide
Midland, TX
915-685-1566

Survivors of Suicide
Plano, TX
214-881-0088

Heartbeat
P.O. Box 60731
San Angelo, TX 76906
915-944-1666
915-655-7479

Survivors of Loved One's Suicide
Ecumenical Center
8310 Ewing Halsell Drive
San Antonio, TX 78229
210-695-9136

UTAH
Legacy
2684 N. 2700 East
Layton, UT 84040
801-771-8476
801-394-5556

SEASONS: Suicide Bereavement
P.O. Box 187
Park City, UT 84060
801-649-8327

Survivors of Suicide
4391 W. 4100 South
West Valley City, UT 84102
801-969-1081

VERMONT
Upper Valley S.O.S.
Hospice VNH
325 Mt. Support Road
Lebanon, NH 03766
(near border NH and VT)
603-448-5182
802-295-2064

VIRGINIA
Survival After Suicide
P.O. Box 74
Dumfries, VA 22026
703-368-4141
703-368-8069

Suicide Survivor Support Group
3601 Devilwood Court
Fairfax, VA 22030
703-866-2100
703-273-3454

Suicide Survivor Support Group
St. Phillips Catholic Church
Falls Church, VA
703-866-2100
703-573-3808

Survivors of Suicide Support Group
Hospice Support Care
2119 Lafayette Boulevard
Fredericksburg, VA 22401
540-710-0480

Healing After Suicide
305 N. 4th Avenue
Hopewell, VA 23860
804-541-7795
804-458-3895

Suicide Support Group
St. James Episcopal Church
14 Cornwall Street
Leesburg, VA
540-338-5756

Survivors of Suicide
Catholic Charities
12829 Jefferson Avenue, Ste. 101
Newport News, VA 23608
757-875-0060
757-591-2418

Haven of Northern Virginia
Suicide Survivor Group
703-741-9000

Survivors of Suicide
St. Andrews Lutheran Church
4811 High Street, West
Portsmouth, VA 23707
804-483-5111

West End Behavioral Healthcare System
12800 W. Creek Parkway
Richmond, VA 23238
804-784-6774

S.O.S.
347 Tomahawk Trail
Virginia Beach, VA 23454

Suicide For Those Who Remain
4219 Ben Gunn Road
Virginia Beach, VA 23455
804-464-1513

Survivors of Suicide
Winchester, VA
540-667-1178

Survivors of Suicide Group
Fauquier Hospital
500 Hospital Drive
Warrenton, VA
540-347-5922

WASHINGTON
King Co. S.O.S.
Bible Baptist Church
1320 Auburn Way-South
Auburn, WA 98002
206-833-7127

Survivors Of Suicide
18415 104th Avenue NE
Bothell, WA 98011
425-487-3355

Care Crisis Line/ S.O.S.
Volunteers of America Care Crisis Line
P.O. Box 839
Everett, WA 98206
206-316-3536

Survivors of Suicide
Tri-Cities Chaplaincy
2108 W. Entiat Avenue
Kennewick, WA 99336
509-783-7416

Snamonish Co. S.O.S.
1300 Mice Creek Boulevard
Mice Creek, WA 98012
206-316-3536

Survivors Of Suicide
Crisis Line Of King Co.
1515 Dexter Ave. North, Ste. 300
Seattle, WA 98109
206-461-3210
206-461-3222

Renton/ Seattle S.O.S.
12044 59th Avenue South
Seattle, WA 98178
206-772-5141

Survivors Of A Loved One's
Suicide
East 1933 Illinois
Spokane, WA 99207
509-838-4428
509-483-3310

Tacoma S.O.S.
Greater Lakes Mental Health
9108 Lakewood Drive, SW
Tacoma, WA 98499
206-581-6200

Thurston Co. Survivors Group
Institute for Suicide Prevention
9108 Lakewood Drive, SW
Tacoma, WA 98499
360-438-6887
360-422-2552

WEST VIRGINIA
Heartbeat
2900 1st Avenue
St. Mary's Hospital
Huntington, WV 25702
304-526-6014

Survivors Of Suicide
107 Lee Street
Ripley, WV 25721
304-372-4290
304-372-3493

Suicide Survivors Support Group
P.O. Box 4043
Warwood Post Office
Wheeling, WV 26003
304-277-3916

WISCONSIN
Fox Valley- Survivors of Suicide
Appleton, WI
414-739-1231

Suicide Survivors Support Group
Sacred Heart Hospital
1010 Oakridge Drive
Eau Claire, WI 54701
715-833-6028

Survivors Of Suicide
N.E. Wisconsin/ Upper Peninsula
Michigan
630 Greene Avenue
Green Bay, WI 54301
414-437-7527

Karis Support Group
Gundersen-Lutheran Memorial
Center
1910 South Avenue
La Crosse, WI 54601
608-785-0530

Survivors of Suicide
Emergency Services MHC of
Dane Co.
625 West Washington Avenue
Madison, WI 53703
608-280-2600

Survivors of Suicide Support
Group
Pastoral Care Dept./ St. Joseph's
Hospital
611 St. Joseph Avenue
Marshfield, WI 54449
715-387-7753

Appendix 1: Suicide Survivor Organizations

Survivors Helping Survivors
Mental Health Association in
Milwaukee City
734 N. Fourth Street, Ste. 325
Milwaukee, WI 53203
414-276-3122

Suicide Loss Support Group
MHA in Sheboygan Co.
2020 Erie Avenue
Sheboygan, WI 53081
920-458-3951
920-564-3676

Survivors of Suicide
1540 28th Street North
Wisconsin Rapids, WI 54494
715-421-1942
715-421-8600

WYOMING
Share and Care Group
1108 West 27th Street
Cheyenne, WY 82001
307-637-3753
307-638-8642

CANADA BY PROVINCE

ALBERTA
Canadian Mental Health Assoc.
Suicide Services
723 14th Street NW #103
Calgary, AB T2N 2A4
Canada
403-297-1744

Fellowship of Suicide Survivors
Calgary, AB
403-283-6812
403-228-7943

Suicide Bereavement
The Support Network
#301- 11456 Jasper Avenue
Edmonton, AN T5K 0M1
Canada
403-482-0198

L.O.S.S.
13308- 91 Street
Edmonton, AB T5E 3P8
Canada
403-476-7035

Some Other Solutions Society for Crisis Prevention
9912 Manning Avenue
Fort McMurray, AB T9H 2B9
Canada
403-743-8605

BRITISH COLUMBIA
Support Group
6986 Dickinson Road
Lantzville, BC V0R 2H0
Canada
250-390-2865

Survivors of Suicide
Nanaimo, BC
Canada
604-758-3190

S.A.F.E.R.
300, 2425 Quebec Street
Vancouver, BC V5T 4L6
Canada
604-879-9251

NOVA SCOTIA
Springhill Ray Of Hope
P.O. Box 2391
Springhill, NS B0M 1X0
Canada
902-597-3611

ONTARIO
Distress Centre Hamilton
P.O. Box 57317
Jackson SN.A
Hamilton, ON L8P 4X2
Canada
905-525-8611 or 8612

Suicide Bereavement Support Group
Canadian Mental Health Association
648 Huron Street
London, ON N5Y 4J8
Canada
519-434-9199

Survivor Support Program
10 Trinity Square
Toronto, ON M5G 1B1
Canada
416-595-1716

Bereavement Resources
Canadian Mental Health
Association
1400 Windsor Avenue
Windsor, ON N8X 3L9
Canada
519-255-7440

PROVINCE OF QUEBEC
Carrefour Intervention Suicide
C.P. 71
Sherbrooke, PQ J1H 5H5
Canada
819-821-4661
819-564-1664

Centre De Prevention Du Suicide
C.P. 993
Chicoutimi, PQ G7H 5G4
Canada
418-545-9110

Suicide-Action Montreal
2345 Belanger East
Montreal, PQ H2G 1C9
Canada
514-723-4000

Centre De Prevention Du Suicide
1535 Chemin de Foi, Ste. 100
Quebec, PQ G1S 2P1
Canada
418-525-4588
418-683-0933

Centre de Prevention du Suicide
Saguenay-Lac-St.-Jean, PQ
Canada
418-545-1919

APPENDIX- 2
Resources for Information

American Association of Suicidology
The American Association of Suicidology (AAS) is dedicated to the understanding and prevention of suicide. AAS promotes research, public awareness programs, education and training for professionals and volunteers. In addition, it serves as a national clearinghouse for information on suicide.

American Association of Suicidology
4201 Connecticut Avenue, N.W., Suite 408
Washington, DC 20008
202-237-2280
202-237-2282 Fax
www.suicidology.org

American Foundation for Suicide Prevention
The American Foundation for Suicide Prevention (AFSP) is dedicated to advancing our knowledge of suicide and our ability to prevent it. AFSP's activities include: supporting research projects that help further the understanding and treatment of depression and the prevention of suicide; providing information about depression and suicide; promoting professional education for the recognition and treatment of depressed and suicidal individuals; publicizing the magnitude of the problems of depression and suicide and the need for research, prevention and treatment; supporting programs for suicide survivor treatment, research and education.

American Foundation for Suicide Prevention
120 Wall Street, 22nd Floor
New York, NY 10005
888-333-2377
212-363-6237 Fax
www.afsp.org

Anxiety Disorders Association of America
The Anxiety Disorders Association of America (ADAA) promotes the prevention and cure of anxiety disorders and works to improve the lives of all people who suffer from them. The association is made up of professionals who conduct research and treat anxiety disorders and individuals who have a personal or general interest in learning more about such disorders.

Anxiety Disorders Association of America
11900 Parklawn Drive, Suite 100
Rockville, MD 20852
301-231-9350
301-231-7392 Fax
www.adaa.org

Center for Disease Control and Prevention-National Center for Injury Prevention and Control
The National Center for Injury Prevention and Control (NCIPC) works to reduce morbidity, disability, mortality, and costs associated with injuries.

National Center for Injury Prevention and Control
Mailstop K65
4770 Buford Highway N.E.
Atlanta, GA 30341
770-488-1506
770-488-1667 Fax
www.cdc.gov/ncipc

Child and Adolescent Bipolar Foundation
The Child and Adolescent Bipolar Foundation (CABF) is a parent-led, not-for-profit, web-based membership organization. CABF was founded by a national steering committee of concerned parents active in BPParents, an Internet support group. CABF's on-line community includes parents, researchers, medical doctors, neuroscientists, social workers, therapists, civic leaders, teachers, and others.

Child & Adolescent Bipolar Foundation
1187 Wilmette Avenue
P.M.B. #331
Wilmette, IL 60091
847-256-8525
847-920-9498 Fax
www.cabf.org
www.bpkids.org

Depression and Related Affective Disorders Association
The mission of the Depression and Related Affective Disorders Association (DRADA) is to alleviate the suffering arising from depression and manic depression by assisting self-help groups, providing education and information, and lending support to research programs. DRADA works in cooperation with the Department of Psychiatry at the Johns Hopkins University School of Medicine to ensure that materials are medically accurate, as well as to co-sponsor annual mood disorders research/education symposiums. DRADA is a member-based, non-profit organization.

Depression and Related Affective Disorders Association
The Johns Hopkins Hospital, Meyer 3-181
600 North Wolfe Street
Baltimore, MD 21287
410-955-4647
410-614-3241 Fax
www.med.jhu.edu/drada

Health Resources and Services Administration
The Health Resources and Services Administration (HRSA) directs national health programs that improve the Nation's health by assuring equitable access to comprehensive, quality health care for all. HRSA is an Agency of the U.S. Department of Health and Human Services.
hrsa.dhhs.gov

National Alliance for Research on Schizophrenia and Depression

The National Alliance for Research on Schizophrenia and Depression (NARSDAD) is the largest donor-supported organization in the world devoted exclusively to supporting scientific research on brain and behavior disorders. NARSDAD was founded in 1986 by the National Alliance for the Mentally Ill, the National Mental Health Association, the National Depressive and Manic Depressive Association and the Schizophrenia Foundation (now disbanded).

National Alliance for Research on Schizophrenia and Depression
60 Cutter Mill Road, St. 404
Great Neck, NY 11201
516-829-0091
516-487-6930 Fax
www.mhsource.com/narsdad

National Alliance for the Mentally Ill

The National Alliance for the Mentally Ill (NAMI) focuses its efforts on support to persons with serious brain disorders and to their families; advocacy for nondiscriminatory and equitable federal, state, and private sector policies; research into the causes, symptoms and treatments for brain disorders; and education to eliminate the pervasive stigma surrounding severe mental illness.

National Alliance for the Mentally Ill
200 North Glebe Road, St. 1015
Arlington, VA 22203
800-950-6264 Help line
703-524-7600 Front desk
703-524-9094 Fax
www.nami.org

National Depressive and Manic-Depressive Association

The National Depressive and Manic-Depressive Association (National DMDA) is a not-for-profit organization established to educate parents, families, and the public concerning the nature and management of depressive and manic-depressive illness as treatable diseases. The National DMDA fosters self-help for patients and families, and seeks to eliminate discrimination and stigma associated with depressive and manic-depressive illnesses. It also aims to improve access to professional care and to advocate research toward the elimination of depressive and manic-depressive illnesses.

National Depressive and Manic-Depressive Association
730 North Franklin Street, St. 501
Chicago, IL 60610
800-826-3632
312-642-7243
www.ndmda.org

National Institute on Alcohol Abuse and Alcoholism

The National Institute on Alcohol Abuse and Alcoholism (NIAAA) supports and conducts biomedical and behavioral research on the causes, consequences, treatment, and prevention of alcoholism and alcohol-related problems. NIAAA also leads the national effort to reduce the severe and often fatal consequences of these problems by conducting and supporting research directed at determining the causes of alcoholism, supporting and conducting research across a wide range of scientific areas through the awarding of grants and within the NIAAA intramural research program. The NIAAA also conducts policy studies and epidemiological studies, while collaborating with other research institutes and Federal programs relevant to alcohol abuse and alcoholism.

National Institute on Alcohol Abuse and Alcoholism
6000 Executive Boulevard, Willco Building
Bethesda, MD 20892
www.niaaa.nih.gov

National Institute of Mental Health
The National Institute of Mental Health (NIMH) develops the Nation's Strategic Plan for future Brain and Behavioral Research. A wide variety of initiatives takes place, based on NIMH's comprehensive scientific and administrative platform. Special priority is given to Childhood Mental Disorders Research programs. The NIHM expanded its public education and prevention information dissemination programs, including information on suicide, eating disorders, and panic disorder.

National Institute of Mental Health
6001 Executive Boulevard
Bethesda, MD 20892
800-421-4211
www.nimh.nih.gov

National Institute of Mental Health Suicide Research Consortium
The National Institute of Mental Health (NIMH) Suicide Research Consortium is comprised mainly of NIMH scientists across the Institute who also administer research grants. The Consortium coordinates program development in suicide research across the Institute, identifies gaps in the scientific knowledge base on suicide across the life span, stimulates and monitors extramural research on suicide, keeps abreast of scientific developments in suicidology and public policy issues related to suicide surveillance, prevention and treatment, and disseminates science-based information on suicidology to the public, media, and policy makers.
www.nimh.nih.gov/research/suicide.htm

National Institute on Drug Abuse
The mission of the National Institute on Drug Abuse (NIDA) is to lead the Nation in bringing the power of science to bear on drug abuse and addiction. This charge has two critical components: the first is the strategic support and conduct of research across a broad range of disciplines. The second is to ensure the rapid and effective dissemination and use of the results of that research to significantly improve drug abuse and addiction prevention, treatment and policy.

National Institute on Drug Abuse
National Institutes of Health
6001 Executive Boulevard
Bethesda, MD 20892
800-644-6432
www.nida.nih.gov

National Mental Health Association

The National Mental Health Association (NMHA) is the country's oldest and largest non-profit organization addressing all aspects of mental health and mental illness. With more than 340 affiliates nationwide, NHMA works to improve the mental health of all Americans, especially the 54 million individuals with mental disorders, through advocacy, education, research and service.

National Mental Health Association
1201 Prince Street
Alexandria, VA 22314
800-969-6642
703-684-5968 Fax
www.nmha.org

Screening for Mental Health, Inc. (SMH)
(formerly: National Mental Illness Screening Project)

Screening for Mental Health (SMH) is a non-profit organization developed to coordinate nationwide mental health screening programs and to ensure cooperation, professionalism, and accountability in mental illness screenings. SMH screening days and programs include: National Alcohol Screening Day (NASD), National Anxiety Disorder Screening Day (NADSD), National Depression Screening Day (NDSD), National Eating Disorders Screening Day (NEDSP), Interactive Screening for the Workplace and Healthcare Companies, and Suicide Education and Research Division.

Screening for Mental Health, Inc. (SMH)
One Washington Street, St. 304
Wellesley Hills, MA 02481
800-573-4433 Depression Screening
781-431-7447 Fax
www.nmisp.org

Substance Abuse and Mental Health Services
Substance Abuse and Mental Health Services (SAMHSA) is the Federal agency charged with improving the quality and availability of prevention, treatment, and rehabilitative services in order to reduce illness, death disability, and cost to society resulting from substance abuse and mental illnesses. SAHMSA is an Agency of the U.S. Department of Health and Human Services.
www.samhsa.gov

Suicide Prevention Advocacy Network
The Suicide Prevention Advocacy Network (SPANUSA) is dedicated to the creation and implementation of effective national suicide prevention strategies based on the 1999 Surgeon General's Call To Action To Prevent Suicide.

Suicide Prevention Advocacy Network
5034 Odin's Way
Marietta, GA 30068
888-649-1366
770-642-1419
www.spanusa.org

Surgeon General of the United States
The website contains information about Surgeon General Dr. David Satcher's National Strategy for Suicide Prevention.
www.surgeongeneral.gov